Mainstreaming
in the
Social Studies

John G. Herlihy and Myra T. Herlihy, Editors

National Council for the Social Studies • Bulletin 62

National Council for the Social Studies

Library of Congress Catalog Card Number: 80-81636
ISBN 0-87986-026-X
Copyright © 1980 by the
NATIONAL COUNCIL FOR THE SOCIAL STUDIES
3615 Wisconsin Ave., N.W. Washington, D.C. 20016

Contents

About the Authors

Sandra Alper is Associate Professor of Special Education at the University of Missouri in Columbia. She is currently directing a federally funded project designed to develop a model of community-based, vocational service delivery for severely handicapped youth.

Edward Rockoff is Research Associate at Educational Adaptations in St. Augustine, Florida. He has been an Assistant Professor at Glassboro State in New Jersey and Miami University of Ohio with a specialty in mental retardation. He has also been a consultant for school systems with projects relating to least restrictive placements.

George P. Gregory is Associate in Curriculum Development at the State Education Department, Albany, New York. He was Assistant Professor of Education at the State University College of Arts and Science at Geneseo, New York, with a specialty in social studies education. He has published articles on mainstreaming in the social studies in *The Directive Teacher* and *Social Education.*

Howard Sanford is Assistant Professor of Special Education at the State University College of Arts and Science at Geneseo, New York. He has authored an article on mainstreaming in the social studies in *Social Education.* His area of specialty is curriculum development in special education.

Robert L. Marion is Associate Professor of Special Education at the University of Texas at Austin. He has worked in the areas of career/vocational planning and parent education. His expertise is working with culturally diverse families.

Ramon M. Rocha is Assistant Professor of Special Education at the State University College of Arts and Science at Geneseo, New York. His area of specialty is mental retardation. He has published an article on mainstreaming in the social studies in *Social Education* and will deliver a mainstreaming presentation on this topic at the 1980 conference of the Council for Exceptional Children.

Thomas M. Skrtic is Assistant Professor of Special Education and Curriculum Instruction at the University of Kansas in Lawrence. He teaches graduate and undergraduate courses on mainstreaming. He was also a resource room teacher in a mainstreamed school system.

Frances L. Clark is a Research Assistant in the Institute for Research in Learning Disabilities at the University of Kansas in Lawrence. She has been a classroom teacher and is working on her doctoral dissertation in the area of measurement of attitudes towards exceptional children.

H. Earle Knowlton is Assistant Professor of Special Education at the University of Kansas at Lawrence. His area of specialty is learning disabilities. He teaches graduate courses and conducts inservice programs to prepare regular and special educators for mainstreaming.

William T. Lowe is Professor of Education and Chairperson of the Center for the Study of Curriculum and Teaching at the University of Rochester, Rochester, New York. His areas of specialty are social studies education, curriculum theory, and political sociology. He has authored many articles on social studies education and was book review editor of *Social Education* (1972-75).

John G. Herlihy is Acting Chairperson of the Department of Elementary and Secondary Education at the State University College of Arts and Science at Geneseo, New York. He has taught social studies in junior and senior high schools, directed National Science Foundation grants in social studies curriculum implementation, and taught social studies methods classes at the college level. He has edited and authored articles on mainstreaming in the social studies in *Social Education* and made presentations on the topic at NCSS conferences.

Myra T. Herlihy is Instructor in the Department of Elementary and Secondary Education at the State University College of Arts and Science at Geneseo, New York. She has taught social studies in junior and senior high schools, worked in social studies curriculum implementation in National Science Foundation grants, and taught general and social studies methods and supervised elementary and social studies student teachers at the college level. She was a member of the Board of Advisors for the Elementary Education Section of *Social Education* (1974-1980) and has co-authored and edited articles on mainstreaming in the social studies in *Social Education*.

Foreword

When I was a boy in rural California school districts, mainstreaming was not an issue; it was a reality. Young people who were handicapped, but who could still take part in regular classrooms, were always part of the school environment with which I was familiar. In our infinite wisdom as educators, special programs seemed a more appropriate way to deal with the handicapped; and for years, special classes and schools have been used to provide such youngsters with educational opportunities out of the mainstream. Certainly, by their isolation, these programs limited the extent to which handicapped young people learned to make their way in our chaotic and confusing American mainstream.

In keeping with the broad-based efforts throughout our society to provide equal opportunity for all people, it is appropriate to question the degree to which special schools and classes provide an appropriate education for the handicapped. Certainly, there are those who are so severely limited physically or emotionally that they could not take part in any aspect of a regular school program. However, there are many young people who could profit from and become better able to participate in American life if they had the opportunity to learn as students of regular schools.

The most recent step toward mainstreaming handicapped youngsters came with the passage of Public Law 94-142 and with appropriations to make its implementation possible by school districts throughout America. We are now in the midst of implementing this mainstreaming legislation, and we can now see the differences between the ideal of equal educational opportunity and the reality of providing young people with "the least restrictive environment" in which they can learn. As is often the case, there is a broad gap between the principle of mainstreaming and the task itself. For the beleaguered classroom teacher, mainstreaming represents yet another task to be carried out with enthusiasm, dedication, sophistication, and commitment. Social studies teachers are not alone, since this same expectation exists for all who teach. Nevertheless, basic skills and competencies, the obvious needs of young people for assistance in dealing with a number of social problems that exist in America today, and new requirements for mainstreaming do not please many overburdened teachers. Even with abundant federal money, mainstreaming will only succeed if teachers see significant gains for their students and themselves as a result of this change in school organization. If mainstreaming remains a difficult burden for teachers, or if the requirements of the public law as implemented are troublesome or contradictory to tasks to which teachers give a higher priority, then this change in school organization will not succeed.

This Bulletin, prepared by individuals of broad experience at the task of mainstreaming, is intended to give social studies teachers practical help with the difficult tasks required. Even with this book, mainstreaming will not be easy. However, the advice it gives is sound, and I hope that teachers will consult it carefully as they work to carry out this important challenge: To provide equal opportunity for all our citizens.

Todd Clark, *President*
National Council for the Social Studies

Preface

In any human endeavor, interaction and support are key elements in seeing that effort through to completion. This Bulletin is no exception. The editors wish to express their appreciation for contributions made to the design, organization, selection of authors, and critical review of the manuscript. Specifically, we wish to thank George Gregory, Ramon Rocha, Howard Sanford, and John Youngers for helping us to maintain our energies and focus in developing this Bulletin.

Partial support for the preparation of this book came from the Geneseo Foundation. The Foundation is a nonprofit organization that helps support faculty research and dissemination of publications. We are particularly grateful to the Foundation's Executive Secretary, Fred Bennett, retired; Arthur Hatton, present Executive Secretary; and the Board of Directors for their interest in and support of this Bulletin.

The task of orchestrating eleven chapters with eleven different authors from five states posed problems of integration and timetables. We were fortunately blessed with a group of dedicated professionals who met deadlines, calmly accepted suggestions for revisions, and expended time, effort, and care in developing and polishing their manuscripts. We wish to thank them for a high quality performance.

We dedicate this Bulletin both to handicapped children and to their teachers, who will make mainstreaming a functional reality. For the teacher, we wish courage, inspiration, and patience. For the handicapped child, we wish a successful mainstreaming experience.

John G. Herlihy and Myra T. Herlihy, *Editors*

Mainstreaming
in the
Social Studies

"... handicapped students will have a range of options and alternatives to increase their opportunities for success in a classroom."

I. Why Mainstreaming?

John G. Herlihy and Myra T. Herlihy

The principle of mainstreaming has potential for radically reorganizing schools, instruction, organizational design, classroom learning environments, and the roles and expectations for teachers and students. Mainstreaming also encompasses another set of dimensions—the direct involvement with and approval of parents in instructional decisions that affect their children.

Mainstreaming applies the principle of inclusion as opposed to exclusion of students with handicapping conditions. Essentially this means that students will be involved in the mainstream (regular classroom). Children with handicapping conditions historically have been placed in isolated situations with varying degrees of geographic and emotional distance from regular classrooms. As a result, the social and emotional interactions that are a part of the major socializing agency of American youth—the public schools—have not been available to handicapped youngsters. This isolation was in the form of separate special education classes in a school or in a residential institution a considerable distance from school or home.

Mainstreaming does not mean wholesale dumping of children who were previously not a part of schools on unsuspecting teachers. If it did, it might result in failure for the handicapped students and frustration and anxiety on the part of teachers. Rather, [mainstreaming relates to providing the maximum degree of participation and inclusion for handicapped students, either full or part time, according to their ability to profit from a "regular" setting.] Thus, a major alternative to the lockstep for all students is presented. This different use of time, instruction, and cooperative support will produce significant changes in instructional processes and systems. A discussion of the definition of mainstreaming and the nature of the handicapped population is the focus of Chapter 2. At this point, the reader should be alerted to a few key phrases or words that constitute the essence of the term. They are: zero rejection, parent advocacy, least restrictive environment, individual education program, individual education plan, and anti-labeling or anti-categorization.

Social studies will undoubtedly be in the forefront of areas affected by mainstreaming, for it is a general education subject in the school curricula. Highly specific areas, such as reading and mathematics, have had a history of sequence-skill development and group work. These basic skill areas will be marginally affected, as they have already developed service and delivery systems that facilitate individual or small-group instruction. Social studies, on the other hand, is perceived as a general subject area, and, as such, is often offered to every student at every grade level in total class settings. Of all the subject areas in the curriculum, social studies will surely be one of the first major subject areas to implement mainstreaming. Therefore, social studies teachers must be prepared to deal with the different set of values, training, and operations that are inherent in this evolving force in schools.

The number of students who are to be mainstreamed requires a degree of clarification. Experts[1] state that approximately five per cent of the school-age population falls into handicapping areas requiring special environments. Almost all of these students are not able to function in a school setting. An additional ten to twelve per cent need a form of special services regularly. This group will be able to participate in a limited way (in varying time periods and with support services) in a regular classroom. These children are the population targeted for mainstreaming. It is further estimated that an additional twenty-five per cent of a class will be involved in some form of out-of-class intervention to assist in remediating some aspect of handicapping at some time during their elementary years (K-6). This population is categorized as Learning Disabled (LD)—which indicates a type of impediment to the teaching-learning process (visual and auditory perceptual problems, speech deficiencies, physical handicaps, or behavior problems).

[The essential facts to remember are: (1) mainstreamed students will not be placed en masse in a classroom, (2) the teacher will be provided with information on the nature of the handicap and the remediations to be followed, and (3) support team/systems will assist the teacher in designing and carrying out proper remedial interventions. These elements emphasize the need for the existence of functioning support systems for both teacher and student. [Chapter 3 of this Bulletin is devoted to naming, describing, and demonstrating these mechanisms in operation.

In brief, it is evident that social studies teachers will be in the forefront of any implementation of mainstreaming. Considering the legislation, legal opinions and mandates, and parent advocacy that have generated and supported mainstreaming, it is in the best self-interests of social studies teachers, K-12, to become knowledgeable about the aims and goals of mainstreaming. Educators also should become familiar with the support systems that will furnish assistance to implement that idea successfully in their classrooms.

Mainstreaming is a difficult concept to reduce to a definition. It is more an attitudinal or value-oriented position that allows the teacher to examine each child and provide an appropriate way to develop, expand, and refine the student's intellectual, social, and emotional skills. Numerous references to definitions can be made, but they all reflect the need to treat, in an educational setting, every child in a way that will promote his or her intellectual and emotional health. The notion of the least restrictive environment supports this concept by requiring that appropriate settings be found—these educational settings can have varying time dimensions, locales, instructional components, and people—for handicapped pupils. As a result, handicapped students will have a range of options and alternatives to increase their opportunities for success in a classroom. Teachers will find a new set of conditions operating in their classrooms as ancillary personnel and out-of-class settings (resource rooms are one example) are used. One source lists a number of resources involved in the shared responsibility required to mainstream successfully.[2] They are: regular teacher, special education teacher, director of special education, principal, counselors, school psychologist, librarians, therapists, paraprofessionals, students, parents, community volunteers, and professional organizations. This plethora of resources suggests the end of the isolation of a teacher and 30 pupils in a classroom. In its place, there is a team approach orchestrated by the teacher to fill the needs of all children.

Handicapping is a descriptive not a definitional term, and the range and variety of conditions involved are great. For ease in categorizing, one author offers five general groupings of handicapping.[3] They are: cognitive, physical, communicative, sensory, and emotional/behavioral. From inspection, it is evident that most handicapped children in a teacher's classroom will have deficiencies in collecting or processing data, but they will not be incapable of learning. Hard-core cases which would not benefit socially, emotionally, or cognitively will not be included in mainstreaming. This Bulletin is directed at those handicapping conditions that create blockage or hindrance to traditional instructional modes and practices. These are conditions that affect the mainstreamed children who will be in the teacher's classroom.

This Bulletin is directed, too, to discussing the implications of mainstreaming for social studies teachers, K-12. The organization of the book, as seen by the chapter titles, stresses two ideas. The first underscores the need for support/delivery systems to assist both teachers and students. The second provides numerous examples of successful classroom practices and lessons to point out the integration of the support systems. The task of implementing mainstreaming in social studies classrooms is going to be difficult and time-consuming. This Bulletin is an attempt to demonstrate that it can be done and is being done.

P.L. 94-142

Mainstreaming has many antecedents. Treatment of and provision for handicapped youngsters has gone through many metamorphoses: from neglect, to isolation (residential setting), to special classes, and now to progressive inclusion. A brief description of these periods is found in the writings of Rocha and Sanford[4] and a more comprehensive treatment is found in Reynolds and Birch.[5] This history reflects a number of changes in values and attitudes from non-awareness, to acceptance of charitable beneficence of society, to the present thrust of aggressive assertion of rights. This assertion is reflected in cases in the courts, in legislation, in organized political action and lobbying, and in repeated applications of due process in an effort to obtain the rights of children for full participation in the mainstream of American society. Political and legal testing generated the force that resulted in the "Education for all Handicapped Children Act of 1975"—P.L. 94-142. This legislation is called the Bill of Rights for the handicapped and is the basis for mainstreaming. The major components of P.L. 94-142 are:

1. a full service goal (free public education for all handicapped children, ages 3-21, by September 1, 1980).
2. due process safeguards (these apply to all phases of identification, placement, and evaluation).
3. least restrictive environment (handicapped children are to be placed with the non-handicapped as much as possible).
4. non-discriminatory testing and evaluation (selection and administration of tests and procedures must be appropriate for the handicapping condition and racially and culturally non-discriminatory).
5. individualized education plans (developed and annually reviewed by teachers, parents, and a designee of the school district for each identified handicapped child).
6. personnel development (a system must be developed to train regular and special teachers and administrators to implement the law).[6]

From this brief summary of the highlights of the law, it can be seen that stress is placed on due process, parental involvement, anti-labeling or anti-categorizing, development of IEPs, placement in the least restrictive environment, cooperative action between federal, state, and local education agencies, multi-factorial assessment (non-discriminatory testing), and annual review of education plans.[7] The law calls for free and appropriate public education for all handicapped children who can benefit, even for a short time or under limited conditions, from placement in regular classrooms.

Four Rationales

The very nature of this legislation provides a means to look at the larger society—an action that is at the heart of social studies education. Since mainstreaming is an attitudinal or value orientation, a number of rationales that provide the philosophic assumptions of the law have been offered. These positions have direct application for social studies educators, K-12. A review of the literature reveals four basic positions in support of the concept.

• **The most frequently cited argument in support of mainstreaming relates to the struggle for the extension of civil rights.** This has clearly been seen in black suffrage; busing (both in seating arrangements and as a means of achieving racial balance); and, most visibly, in the Supreme Court ruling that the doctrine of separate but equal treatment in education is unconstitutional. Other groups—women, the aged, and others—have also actively battled and conducted political action in order to secure similar civil rights. The parallel of separate but equal treatment to the handicapped is clear. If exclusion, isolation, and separation are illegal by race, then exclusion, isolation, and separation by handicapping condition must be just as injurious and illegal. An examination of this tenet applied to handicapping conditions is an excellent way to conduct a set of concept development lessons relating to such social studies topics/area/content as: the role of minorities, the elements of social change, democracy as an evolving system, and the employment of political power within the system. Thus, classroom activities and events (the advent of handicapped children in a teacher's class, for instance) can be the means to study political problems and issues in the United States today. The rationale offered is that a significant proportion of America's youth has been denied full participation in and benefits from the mainstream of American life; and that, as a result of past practices, it has also been denied the protections of full citizenship rights.

• **A second rationale offered to support mainstreaming relates to the nature, purpose, and composition of our system of free public education.** If a free public education is considered a value, then it must be offered to every child—regardless of handicapping condition. A study, review, and analysis of the nature of free public education will focus attention on questions such as: Who is to be educated? Why was a free public education system established? What are the present and/or past goals of our educational system? This approach will deal with the social studies notion of the dignity and worth of the individual and of that individual's place in the larger social setting or social agency; e.g., the public schools. Related topics, such as education for women and members of minorities, will suggest direct relationships to the goals of mainstreaming. From this approach, it is only a short step to the study of other socializing agencies (family, home, scouts, church, community). A study of this rationale can lead to a functional understanding of major socialization forces and a broader perspective on the multifaceted nature of our society.

• **A third rationale presented by proponents in support of mainstreaming offers the proposition that the classroom should**

become a microcosm of the real world—not an artificial setting that does not reflect the nature and composition of the world the child will enter as an adult. Social interaction, social contact, and social action are the warp and woof of social studies education. The skills, abilities, adaptations, and contributions that handicapped children bring to a classroom will expand the horizons and extend the experiences of all the children. As the classroom becomes more reality-oriented, students will have the opportunity to explore and learn the coping behaviors needed to survive as adults. The classroom then can become a social laboratory for the development and refinement of attitudes and values. Social studies teachers can apply values education techniques, interpersonal com-munication exercises, group-process skills, and self-concept lessons by using the classroom for laboratory experiences related to mainstreaming and handicapping conditions.

• The fourth rationale in support of mainstreaming relates to placing school and schooling in a larger context. A review of the purposes and operation of the law clearly reflects the notion of parent advocacy and community involvement. A class, then, is not viewed as an island of thirty pupils, one teacher, and a textbook surrounded by chalkboards. Rather, education is a system of wider involvement both within and outside of the school building. Since outside agencies—community, political, and volunteer—are involved, the classroom and the school become part of the larger educational/learning environment for the child. For the social studies educator, this provides a mechanism for community analysis and a *raison d'être* for conducting surveys of community resources that will lead all children to better knowledge and understanding of their local government.

In brief, the issues, principles, and prospects of mainstreaming are not amorphous, theoretical constructs. Mainstreaming provides the means for an intensive reflection on the social studies program. Although this effort is devoted to mainstreaming, it will lead to a wider perspective of children, curricula, fellow professionals, and the community; and this, in turn, will result in a stronger social studies program.

Footnotes

[1]Maynard C. Reynolds and Jack W. Birch, *Teaching Exceptional Children in All America's Schools* (Reston, Virginia: The Council for Exceptional Children, 1977), pp. 41-42.

Ann P. Turnbull and Jane B. Schulz, *Mainstreaming Handicapped Students: A Guide for the Classroom Teacher* (Boston: Allyn and Bacon, Inc., 1979), p. 2.

[2]*Ibid.,* pp. 66-72.

[3]*Ibid.,* Chapter 1, "Educational Characteristics of Handicapped Students," pp. 1-48.

[4]Ramon M. Rocha and Howard G. Sanford, "Mainstreaming: Democracy in Action," *Social Education* 43 (January 1979): 60.

[5]Reynolds and Birch, *op. cit.,* pp. 14-23.

[6]Seymour Sarason and John Doris, "The Education for All Handicapped Children Act (Public Law 94-142): What Does It Say?" *Readings in Mainstreaming 78/79* (Guilford, Connecticut: Special Learning Corporation, 1978), p. 183.

[7]For greater detail on the law, see:

a. Council for Exceptional Children's three multimedia packages on the many facets of the law; also a general informational brochure, *The Education for All Handicapped Act-P.L. 94-142.* (See Chapter 11 for details.)

"Education for All Handicapped Children Act of 1975," Public Law 94-142, 94th Congress, S. 6, November 29, 1975.

"There should . . . be social and instructional integration. . . ."

2.What Is Mainstreaming?

Sandra Alper

The purposes of this chapter are to define and describe mainstreaming—what it is as well as what it is not; to discuss problems involved in its implementation; and to provide some examples of how social studies teachers can implement mainstreaming. This chapter is written with the regular classroom teachers in mind. It is upon them that the heaviest burden of implementing mainstreaming ultimately falls.

What Is Mainstreaming?

Simply stated mainstreaming means providing special education services to exceptional children while they remain in regular classes for as much of the day as possible.[1] The term "exceptional" refers to those students whose educational needs require special education services. Included, for example, are students who are mildly retarded, learning disabled, behaviorally disordered, hard of hearing, visually impaired, or physically handicapped.

A more specific definition of mainstreaming is presented by Kaufman, Gottlieb, Agard, and Kubic.[2] According to them, there are three basic components of mainstreaming:

1. Integration
2. Educational planning and programming
3. Clarification of responsibilities

1. Integration. In many cases the "least restrictive setting" (i.e., the setting which is most like that of non-handicapped students) in which a handicapped child may be appropriately educated is the regular classroom. If, after referral and testing, a student is judged able to attend classes with non-handicapped students, rather than being segregated in special groups, that student is transferred to the regular classroom for all, or part, of the school day. However, temporal integration alone—that is, merely placing the exceptional child in a regular class for a period of time—is not sufficient. There should also be *social* and *instructional* integration with non-handicapped peers. A hard-of-hearing student, for example, placed in a regular social studies classroom, should participate in the full range of social and instructional activities available to his non-handicapped peers. The social studies teacher's concern would not necessarily be on giving this student different content, but would, rather, emphasize alternate ways of presenting the same content.

2. Educational Planning and Programming. The educational program of the mainstreamed child needs to be carefully planned. Merely placing a student in a regular classroom is not sufficient. Efforts must be made to plan and program for the unique needs of handicapped students so that they can benefit academically and socially from participation in the regular classroom. In order for this to happen, supportive personnel and services must be available to the child *and* to the regular class teacher. Ideally, the special class teacher should work closely with the social studies teacher as well as with the handicapped child. For example, the special education teacher might provide suggestions to the regular social studies class teacher for methods of presenting a lesson to a class which includes a hearing impaired or visually impaired student. He or she might, in addition, then work with the handicapped student individually in order to reinforce concepts taught in the regular social studies classroom.

3. Clarification of Responsibilities. Unfortunately, in some mainstreaming situations, the regular class teacher has had to assume total responsibility for the handicapped child. Additional special education personnel should also be involved. This might include a resource teacher. When both special and regular education personnel are working with a handicapped child, there may be some confusion over who is responsible for what. These roles must be delineated carefully and clearly so that the child's total needs can be met. For example, the social studies teacher might assume responsibility for presenting some lessons to a learning disabled child through filmstrips or audio tape cassettes, while the resource teacher could assume responsibility for working individually with that child on his or her specific difficulties encountered in verbally identifying words in the social studies reading assignments.

Who Is To Be Mainstreamed?

The term "exceptional children" is commonly used to refer to children with a wide range of sensory, physical, learning, and behavioral characteristics which require some type of special education services. These children may be labeled mentally retarded, learning disabled, behaviorally disordered, visually impaired, hearing impaired, and/or physically handicapped, to name but a few categories used in the field of special education.

The attempt to define and classify handicapped children using these labels is, on the one hand, useful in conveying information for administrative purposes. On the other hand, the lack of specific explanations for what makes a child exceptional and the variability of characteristics found within categories do not allow a single label or category to clarify the learning or behavioral problems of these children.[3] Furthermore, these labels cannot and do not point out effective instructional strategies for these students.

Gardner has provided a description of exceptional children which is more useful to classroom teachers.[4] He characterizes exceptional children as having continuing learning and behavioral difficulties. While, in most respects, similar to all children, the exceptional child merely demonstrates different intensities, durations, and/or combinations of problems that are developmental characteristics of most children. These problems may be highlighted in the social studies class due to the variety of academic skills required and the content areas covered within the social studies.

Some problems reflect behavioral deficits—the child is unable to engage in required academic or social behaviors (limited expressive language, for example). Other problems reflect excessive behaviors—the child engages in behaviors that are inappropriate in time, place, frequency or intensity (for example, frequent temper outbursts in the classroom). These characteristics are exceptional. They tell us that the ordinary instructional program must be modified in order to accommodate the individual learning and behavioral characteristics of these students. From this perspective, the regular social studies lesson is altered to "fit" the needs of the handicapped child.

Problems in Implementing Mainstreaming

It is clear that the definitions of mainstreaming discussed above are ideals. They refer to how mainstreaming *should* be carried out in order for it to work. Mainstreaming has not, as yet, been submitted to much research, however. The efficacy of mainstreaming has not been fully tested. There are fears that it could be another educational fad. To prevent this from happening, it is important that mainstreaming be implemented appropriately. As MacMillan, Jones, and Aloia caution, the *principle* of mainstreaming must be distinguished from its *implementation.*[5] That is, the concept of mainstreaming should not be condemned simply because it has not been appropriately administered in some cases.

MacMillan and Becker have pointed out that another difficulty with mainstreaming is that it has occurred primarily because of legislation, rather than because educators independently recognized the need.[6] Many court decisions in the 1970s supported the contentions that standardized testing has resulted in disproportionate numbers of minority children being placed in special classes, that labeling may well be detrimental, that special classes have not been effective, and that parents should be involved in placement decisions. As MacMillan and Becker noted, the courts have told educators what *not* to do, but they have not indicated what the correct solutions are.[7]

A third problem has been misconceptions of what mainstreaming is or is not. The term "mainstreaming" has been used frequently and in different ways during the last few years. The Council for Exceptional Children has published some basic themes which help to clarify the concept of mainstreaming:[8]

Mainstreaming is:

- providing the most appropriate education for each child in the least restrictive setting.
- looking at the educational needs of children instead of clinical or diagnostic labels such as mentally handicapped, learning disabled, physically handicapped, hearing impaired, or gifted.
- looking for and creating alternatives that will help general educators serve children with learning or adjustment problems in the regular setting. Some approaches being used to help achieve this include the services of consulting teachers, methods and materials specialists, itinerant teachers, and resource room teachers.
- uniting the skills of general education and special education so that all children may have equal education opportunity.

Mainstreaming is not:

- wholesale return of all exceptional children in special classes to regular classes.
- permitting children with special needs to remain in regular classrooms without the support services that they need.
- ignoring the need of some children for a more specialized program than can be provided in the general education program.
- less costly than serving children in special self-contained classrooms.

Finally, one of the biggest problems with the mainstreaming movement has been the assumptions that it can and will be readily embraced by regular classroom teachers. Consequently, some mainstreamed classes have been quickly established with little planning for how to prepare general educators for their new and difficult role. The need for preparing regular class teachers and students for mainstreaming *before* mainstreaming actually occurs is essential. To paraphrase Birch, teachers should be given the tools to work with pupils before being given the pupils:[9]

Approaches to Developing a Mainstreaming Program

The question is no longer "Should we mainstream?" but rather "How do we prepare for mainstreaming?" Birch, after reviewing successful mainstreaming programs in varying parts of the nation, recommended the following key points be considered in implementing such programs.[10]

1. **Regular class and special education teacher concerns need consideration.** Major educational decisions in school systems should not be made without the constructive influence of consultation with teachers. Teachers' attitudes, suggestions, and feedback will influence the success or failure of a program.

2. **Regular class teachers need the opportunity to talk about mainstreaming.** Teachers need to be assured that handicapped children will not be forced into their regular classes, but will be moved in with their full understanding and agreement. Teacher concerns relative to inappropriate classroom behaviors, appropriate instructional materials and techniques, classroom organization, and support services available should be dealt with *before* mainstreaming is implemented.

3. **Teacher attitudes influence mainstream success.** Positive attitudes of teachers can greatly facilitate mainstreamed education.
The attitudes most conducive to success for mainstreaming include the following:

    A. Belief in the right to education for all children.
    B. Readiness of special education and regular class teachers to cooperate with each other.
    C. Willingness to share competencies as a team in behalf of pupils.
    D. Openness to include parents as well as other professional colleagues in planning for and working with children.
    E. Flexibility with respect to class size and teaching assignments.
    F. Recognition that social and personal development can be taught, and that they are equally as important as academic achievement.

4. **Inservice education is a requirement.** Inservice programs should stress the practice of viewing and stating children's educational strengths and weaknesses in functional terms. Expressions such as "She does well in organizing her social studies reports, but needs to learn to write complete sentences and to use basic punctuation" are much more useful to the teacher than are descriptions of children in psychological or medical diagnostic labels.

5. **Keep exceptional pupils in regular grades.** Once placed, mildly handicapped pupils should not be removed from regular classes unless absolutely necessary. Removal can create self-concept problems for the child, problems in understanding and pride for the parents, and problems

of responsibility and resistance to re-entry on the part of regular class teachers. Instead, immediate special education support should be made available to the child and the regular class teacher where they are.

6. Informed parents can be very helpful. Parents should know, understand, and participate in planning. They should have opportunities to react and make suggestions. Parents whose children are in self-contained classes should also have options on whether they wish to have mainstreaming attempted.

7. Emphasize educational assessment and diagnostic teaching. Numerical scores from psychological tests have less impact on classification and school placement decisions for children under mainstreaming conditions. Psychometric test results (e.g., mental ages and intelligence quotients) cannot tell the teacher what or how to teach. Instead, educational assessment plus diagnostic teaching over a period of time can produce information which leads to more credible professional judgments on how to deal with learning problems.

What Can the Regular Social Studies Class Teacher Do?

Lilly, and Hallahan and Kauffman discuss teacher behaviors required for successful mainstreaming.[11] [12]Examples applicable to *many types* of learning problems are:

1. When describing problems of children, *specify observable student behaviors,* rather than labels such as "learning disabled" or "retarded" (e.g., "She can attend to her social studies worksheets for only five minutes at a time," rather than "She can't do the work because she has a learning disability.").

2. The teacher must have *realistic expectations* concerning student performance; tasks should be well within the child's capacity, but still a challenge. If the student is not able to complete a written social studies test satisfactorily, perhaps the task is inappropriate for the child. Students should feel success and pride in what they accomplish. It may be more appropriate to administer the test's content orally to children, to let them demonstrate their mastery of the content through completing a project, or through other assessment procedures.

3. It is essential that the teacher *communicate expectations* to the child clearly and firmly. The child should know what is expected at all times, as well as what the consequences will be for appropriate and inappropriate behaviors.

4. *Set specific achievable objectives* for students with problems in learning and/or social behavior, and teach directly to those objectives.

5. *Continuous assessment* should be made of the stu-

dent's performance. At times, handicapped students' progress may be erratic—up one day, down the next.

6. *Immediate feedback* should be provided to the student for correct as well as incorrect responses.

7. *When giving directions* for completing a task, *observe student responses,* note students who don't follow directions, and, if necessary, alter the content and structure of directions for individual students.

8. For students with minimal reading skills, *provide alternative methods of obtaining information* and taking tests. Information may be gleaned from filmstrips, tape recordings, projects, and class discussions, as well as from texts.

9. Identify students who appear to have low self-concepts, and *program activities aimed at increasing self-confidence.*

10. *Good behavior management* for handicapped children has a lot in common with good behavior management for *all* children. There must be *consistent, appropriate consequences for behavior.* The child's desirable behavior should be immediately recognized and rewarded with praise and other signs of approval. Inappropriate behavior should not be a means by which the child gains attention. Praise for good behavior should be given so that other students can see and hear the teacher's approval. If it is necessary to correct or reprimand the child, this should be done as quietly and *privately* as possible to avoid embarrassment.

11. In *evaluating student performance,* compare the student's present performance to the student's own *previous level* of performance, not to the level of success of other students.

12. When confronted with problems in academic learning or social behavior, *seek advice and help from available resource persons* in the school, without requesting that resource persons assume full responsibility for solutions to the problem.

Conclusion

It is natural that many classroom teachers respond to the prospect of mainstreaming with anxiety. This is a normal expression of concern over the adjustments required when students who will make new kinds of demands and require different approaches are placed in the regular classroom. However, with supportive assistance from special educators, diagnostic specialists, and inservice education programs, the transition can be made and become a positive experience for teachers, handicapped students, and non-handicapped students alike.

Footnotes

[1]Jack Birch, *Mainstreaming: Educable Mentally Retarded Children in the Regular Classes.* (Minneapolis: Leadership Training Institute/Special Education, University of Minnesota, 1974), pp. 2-3.

[2]M. Kaufman, J. Gottlieb, J. Agard, and M. Kubic, "Mainstreaming: Toward an Explication of the Construct," *Focus on Exceptional Children,* 7 (1975): 1-12.

[3]Edward Meyen, *Exceptional Children and Youth* (Denver: Love Publishing Company, 1978), pp. 50-51.

[4]William Gardner, *Children With Learning and Behavioral Problems* (Boston: Allyn and Bacon, Inc., 1978), pp. 43-44.

[5]D. MacMillan, R. Jones, and G. Aloia, "The Mentally Retarded Label: A Theoretical Analysis and Review of Research," *American Journal of Mental Deficiency,* 79 (1974): 241-61.

[6]D. MacMillan and L. Becker, "Mainstreaming the Mildly Handicapped Learner," in R. Kneedler and S.G. Tarver, eds., *Changing Perspectives in Special Education* (Columbus, Ohio: Charles E. Merrill, 1977).

[7]*Ibid.*

[8]*Exceptional Children,* 42, (November, 1975): 174.

[9]Birch, *op. cit.,* pp. 94-5.

[10]*Ibid.,* pp. 88-97.

[11]Steven M. Lilly, "Special Education—A Cooperative Effort," *Theory Into Practice,* 14 (1975): 82-9.

[12]D. Hallahan and J. Kauffman, *Exceptional Children* (Englewood Cliffs, N.J.: Prentice-Hall, Inc., 1978), p. 212.

Resource room teacher, consultant, and chairperson of Committee on the Handicapped.

3. Delivery Systems To Implement Mainstreaming in Social Studies Classrooms

Edward Rockoff

To foster a better understanding of what is happening in education for the handicapped today and why, one must first go back a quarter of a century and review what was happening then. The most popular setting for the handicapped was the self-contained special classroom. The student population was most probably male, mildly retarded, and/or a behavioral problem. There were no special programs or curricula, and the main criterion for the successful class was that it remained quiet and did not disturb the regular classes in the building (unless a segregated building was utilized). Whether or not students in special classes were capable enough to return to their normal classes after a period of time remained a moot question, as most decisions to place a student in special classes were never reconsidered.

Today, we observe things much differently. Most special educators have special education certification. Classrooms utilize appropriate curriculum and materials that have been specially prepared for handicapped students. Having the most quiet classroom is no longer the symbol of a good classroom for the handicapped. Finally, and perhaps more importantly, public education facilities are serving the more severely handicapped student who in the past was totally ignored, forgotten, and/or institutionalized. These changes were brought about primarily by state and federal legislation, particularly P.L. 94-142.

School Personnel Working and Sharing Together

In order to provide the appropriate program to the handicapped child now being served in the regular class, without unnecessary duplication of school services, one must clarify any problems in coordinating roles and disseminating knowledge to personnel. The knowledge a teacher must have to help solve the problems of learning for the exceptional child in the regular classroom is of the utmost importance.

Our educational system is based on people, an obvious fact sometimes overlooked. Administrators (people) administer, teachers (people) teach, and students (people) learn. In order for the system to be effective, all must work together and support each other. Administrators and teachers must be flexible to provide the type of instructional opportunities needed for educating handicapped children in regular classes. Clearly, then, there must be provided to the teachers a preservice education program on the needs of the handicapped student and continual inservice training as well. According to Arthur J. Lewis,[1] the preservice and inservice programs should:

1. help teachers learn the skills and gain the knowledge needed to conduct individualized instruction for all children in a classroom;
2. develop a knowledge of handicapped children that will enable teachers to diagnose learning needs and prescribe appropriate engagements; and
3. develop attitudes toward handicapped children that will enable teachers to approach their task as professionals with compassion, rather than as "do-gooders" with pity.

The following sections are devoted to describing some of the various types of collaborative efforts among adminstrators, regular classroom teachers, and special education persons to provide a service model for the integration of the handicapped student into regular classes.

• Diagnostic-Prescriptive Teacher

The diagnostic-prescriptive teacher (D-P) is an "educational diagnostician-consultant to regular-class teachers in the development of appropriate instructional and socialization experiences for children who are viewed as posing problems in learning and/or behavior."[2]

Diagnostic-prescriptive teaching is the development of a learning situation designed to meet the needs of an individual and his or her unique style of learning. The underlying purpose is to keep the mildly handicapped student in the regular class, rather than placing him or her in a special class. Therefore, when a student seems to be having problems, the blame should not be placed on the child, as is often done, but on the child's educational environment. Rather than placing the child in a stigmatized classroom with others who are labeled, a change in the educational program or a change in the teacher's behaviors may be all that is needed to eliminate the problem the student was believed to have had. In diagnostic-prescriptive teaching, time is taken to create an individually designed program to facilitate the student's learning.

A referral by the regular class teacher, perceiving an academic or behavioral problem in a student, would initiate the process. The child, in most instances, would be referred to a diagnostic-prescriptive teacher or learning disabilities specialist. This person would be concerned with the child, the present classroom situation, the environment, and all the effects these variables have on one another. After consideration of these factors, the D-P teacher would bring the student into his or her class (temporarily) to form and test several educational recommendations. This is a short-term intervention in order to develop an effective program for the individual.

Once the program has been developed, the D-P teacher returns the child to the previous class or to some other most appropriate environment. The D-P teacher helps the regular classroom teacher adjust to the new program by working with the teacher in both settings. The diagnostic-prescriptive teacher never assumes that the regular teacher could interpret and employ the new prescriptive program simply by reading the plan. As needed, the D-P teacher will enter the classroom and work alongside the regular classroom teacher. The case is considered closed when both regular and D-P teachers are satisfied with the child's placement and prescription. Continual periodic checking is undertaken.

For example, suppose a social studies teacher had a student with a deficiency in auditory mode of reception, but the visual mode of reception was well established. The teaching task would be to design a program to strengthen the child's auditory discrimination. Therefore, materials dealing with an auditory output would be utilized which employ visual cues and promote verbal response. The social studies teacher could emphasize board work and worksheets to ensure delivery of facts, concepts, and generalizations to a student with this handicapping condition. Conversely, audio modes, such as lectures and audio tapes, would be de-emphasized with this student.

• Resource Room Teacher Model

The resource room teacher model (non-categorical) should be designed to meet the learning needs of the pupils in the school, not just special education students but normal and gifted as well. Therefore, any student having a difficulty in adjustment or school course work can utilize the resource teacher. One does not have to be in any one classification to obtain needed services.

If the least restrictive alternative is utilized, the special class will accommodate the more severely handicapped student, and the resource room will accommodate the mildly-moderately handicapped whose homeroom would be the normal classroom. In the resource instructional setting, the student participates on a regular part-time schedule. The rest of the school day the student would remain in the regular class.

The resource room teacher is a specially trained professional capable of assessing and planning instruction in problem areas for the student. This teacher is knowledgeable in the areas of special materials and activities that are designed to remediate learning or behavior problems.

The social studies teacher would consult with the resource teacher to determine what content learnings the student needs to acquire in order to function in the regular classroom. For example, the social studies teacher should furnish the resource room teacher with a social studies vocabulary list that a student would need to complete successfully a unit under study in the regular classroom. During the resource room period, the pupil will experience, in a number of appropriate ways, the terms on the list. These *a priori* activities will enable the child to return to the mainstreamed class prepared to cope with the content of the unit.

According to Jenkins and Mayhall,[3] the program in the resource room reflects the principle that a student's participation in the regular classroom depends less on the handicap than on the student's ability to perform the academic tasks selected by the classroom teacher.

• Ancillary Personnel Model

Although educational policy and curriculum have changed in recent years, the classroom teacher still continues to be recognized as the key and/or most important person in the public educational process. If the desired outcomes of education for all children are brought to reality, it will be the classroom teacher who brings them to fruition.

To enhance to the fullest the role of the teacher working with children, most school districts have developed a system of support services. This system may now include speech clinicians, directors of special education, education consultants (curriculum), psychologists, learning disability specialists, and others who might be able to serve as a valuable resource to the classroom teacher as he or she deals with a child who has a learning and/or behavior handicap. Ancillary personnel have two func-tions: (1) to provide direct services to children, and (2) to assist the regular classroom teachers with their specialty area.

Considering all the specialized psycho-educational information that is now available, it is unrealistic to assume that a regular classroom teacher can be a specialist in every possible area. To master the content area of social studies alone seems almost too enormous a feat for one individual to achieve. Thus, the classroom teacher must rely on ancillary resources as a means of obtaining and interpreting specialized information. The teacher should be aware that he or she could be dealing with complex learning problems for which there is no simple solution.[4]

• Itinerant Teacher Model

The itinerant teacher, like the regular classroom teacher, works with students in their regular classroom environment, but the itinerant teacher is only responsible for the one or two identified students and not for the entire class. The itinerant teacher may provide a direct service to the handicapped student or may supplement the instruction of the regular social studies classroom teacher. If a teacher is looking for help with a particular student, a referral would be submitted through proper channels. The itinerant teacher model has been utilized extensively by students who are blind or visually impaired but remain in the regular classroom setting. The itinerant teacher aids the student in learning Braille, making needed classroom materials in Braille, and provides any additional support services needed to help the handicapped student adjust to the regular classroom. For example, it is very difficult, if blind, to understand any aspect of the geography of a country unless the map is 3-D for tactile sensation. The itinerant classroom teacher brings services to the handicapped student in the classroom. This is in contrast to the student utilizing the resource room teacher model where the student comes to the room of the resource teacher. Since the itinerant teacher is in the students' regular classroom, he or she has greater opportunity to discuss and coordinate instruction for the handicapped child with the regular teacher. The itinerant teacher understands the environment of the regular classroom because of the time spent in observation and listening in the classroom.

Discussion and Summary

The four models described in this chapter, designed to assist the teacher in the regular classroom in working with some mildly handicapped students, all involve collaborative relationships between the regular teachers and all of the types of personnel described previously. (See Figure 1.)

Figure 1. Cooperation Is Not a One-way Street.

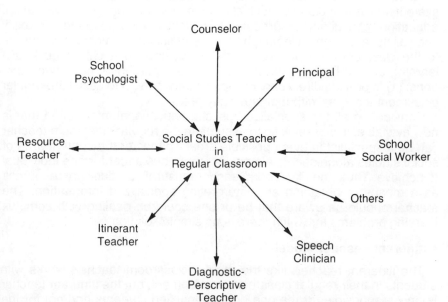

These models are not the only alternatives available. In the future, these models will probably change, or new ones will become available as the needs of different school systems change. The common aspects of all the models are: they are non-categorical in nature; they proceed to analyze the student's problems and devise individualized plans for him or her while maintaining the student in the regular classroom; and they assist the regular classroom teacher with immediate help. Each model proposes a solution to the problems of dissemination of knowledge and role delineation and coordination.

The implementation of these collaborative models to service the mildly handicapped student in the regular classroom might raise questions about teacher certification and program funding. Massachusetts, New Jersey, and Pennsylvania have already made provisions for a more generic certification, and it seems other states will follow.

To service all the children in public education, all professionals must cooperate without regard for level of teaching status. If children are to learn, they will have to be guided by educators dedicated to the principle of the least restrictive environment.

Footnotes

[1]Arthur J. Lewis, "Increased Educational Services to Handicapped Children in Regular Schools," in Maynard Reynolds and M. Davis, eds., *Exceptional Children in Regular Classrooms* (Minneapolis, Minnesota: University Press, 1971), p. 67.

[2]R. Prouty and F.M. McGarry, "The Diagnostic/Prescriptive Teacher," in E. Deno, ed., *Instructional Alternative for Exceptional Children* (Reston, Virginia: The Council for Exceptional Children, 1972), p.47.

[3]J. R. Jenkins and W. F. Mayhall, "Describing Resource Teacher Programs," *Exceptional Children*, 40 (1973): 35-36.

[4]For a more detailed description of how ancillary personnel can be utilized in the regular social studies classroom, the reader is directed to: Edward Rockoff, "Classroom Utilization of Ancillary Personnel," *Social Education*, 43 (January, 1979): 67-68.

". . . mechanisms [provide] for the least restrictive environment, which in reality involves the individualization of instruction."

4.The IEP = Individualization of Instruction

John G. Herlihy and Myra T. Herlihy, editors

Contributors to This Chapter:

Thomas F. Banit
Social Studies Teacher
Walpole High School
Walpole, Massachusetts

Eileen J. Cunningham
Program Coordinator, Special Needs
Sudbury Public Schools
Sudbury, Massachusetts

Mary Ann Bianco
Resource Room Teacher

Lynn Erdle
Resource Room Teacher

Bradley Stanton
Social Studies Teacher

Canandaigua Academy, Canandaigua, New York

Marilyn Gross
Resource Room Teacher
York Central School
Greigsville, New York

Thomas F. Howard
Social Studies Teacher

Alan Waidelich
Resource Room Teacher

Yorktown Heights High School, Yorktown Heights, New York

Public Law 94-142 is the legal mandate for mainstreaming, and it calls for a number of actions that will provide services for handicapped children. Chapter 3 has dealt with mechanisms for providing for the least restrictive environment, which in reality involves the individualization of instruction. The elements of the law and of practice in the field that operationalize this concept focus on the *Individual Educational Program.*

The terminology of the law calls for an Individual Educational Program (IEP). This is defined as "a written statement about the objectives, content, implementation and evaluation of a child's educational program."[1] The IEP is written at least annually; it can (should) be revised more often, if the rate of achievement is greater or less than originally projected. The IEP is cooperatively generated by all—school personnel (regular and special teachers, administrators, ancillary personnel) and parents—who have responsibility for the educational development of the child.

The law requires a program—an overarching design that reflects the intervention that will occur and the anticipated outcomes over a year's time. This program, therefore, is stated in long-range terms, not in short-term units or lesson plans; but these short-term objectives are a part of the larger long-range plan, and collectively they are extremely useful in designing and planning a course. They help to identify or specify where, when, and how parts or a whole section of the IEP are to be achieved. As a result, the term IEP has come to be used for *both* year-long plans and short-term lessons or units. This chapter will use both terms almost interchangeably, since any discussion of operations must include both long-term and short-term aspects of an intervention.

The IEP is a program reflecting what is best for the handicapped child as deemed by professionals and the parents. It is not a legally binding document, but a joint formulation of what educational objectives are proposed for the child, how they are to be attained, and how the results will be evaluated. Another outstanding feature of the IEP is the requirement of participation and approval of the IEP by all parties. The mechanism for this arrangement is the placement committee that must be formed in every K-12 educational enterprise. Parents are a part of this committee and engage in the construction of the IEP that is to be formulated for their child. The law requires close home-school cooperation as well as participation and acceptance of the program and its evaluation by all. As related before, the IEP must be updated at least annually, so the above does not refer to a one-shot or minimum compliance approach.

There are a number of components that are specified in the content of an IEP.[2] A listing, a brief explanation, and implications for social studies teachers are presented to add to teachers' knowledge and understanding of an IEP.

● **The Pupil's Current Educational Status.** This aspect of an IEP relates to developing a full understanding of the achievement profile of the child. Results of formal and standardized tests, informal school reports (grades, files), physical/medical data, and other related materials (reports of ancillary personnel) are assembled. A status report is generated from this data in performance terms that identify academic, physical, and psychological strengths and weaknesses of the child. These base-line data are critical in establishing the areas of need and the nature of the handicapping condition, so that suitable remedial action can be designed. It is important that the data amassed and the reports utilized be accurate and reliable. For the social studies teacher, these status reports will identify the problem areas of learning and will suggest individual approaches to instruction in terms of learning modality, time period, and materials to be used.

• **Statement of Annual Goals.** Each subject area must be reflected in the IEP, and the course goals must be stated in student behavioral outcomes. The goals are for a year's time—or for a semester's, if this is the term of the course—and reflect the content or academic discipline involved. Every social studies teacher is to engage in this activity, which specifies the learning outcomes for pupils in behavioral terms. This task must be completed and forwarded to the placement committee before the course commences. Social studies goals will undoubtedly be stated as evidence of acquisition and application of concepts (representative government, checks and balances, balance of power, nationalism, socialization, opportunity costs) and the utilization of decision-making skills (research, data collecting, analysis, hypothesis formation and testing).

• **Instructional Objectives.** The IEP must contain a step-by-step process for securing instructional goals. These goals may be in content and social studies skills, or they may be related to remediation of the handicapping condition. As a result, they are the formative elements (short-time span) that collectively represent the way in which goals stated in the previous section are to be achieved. For the social studies teacher, this will require breaking down the concept into a number of sub-sets: prior learnings, concept formation exercises, concept development patterns. This is also true for dividing decision making into component parts, such as: research skills, interviewing, observation skills, and communication skills (written and oral).

• **Instructional and Service Requirements.** The existence of a handicapped child in the classroom generally means that out-of-class assistance will be required to provide a success climate for both teacher and student. This element of the IEP is addressed to that need; it ensures that the support services and ancillary personnel needed to staff the services will be involved in the instructional design. The range and variety, as well as the degree, of these services will depend, of course, upon the handicapping condition involved. The major options available are listed and explained in Chapter 3. For the social studies teacher, this will involve consulting with others concerning appropriate intervention: the content involved (resource room), or support instruction (itinerant teacher), or special equipment (raised relief maps for the blind), or special facilities (audio support for the deaf). The key for the social studies teacher is preplanning and an advance notification schedule of support needs.

- **Degree and Nature of Mainstreaming.** The duration and the nature of the support service required in the IEP will depend upon the conditions involved. Many students may need to be out of class receiving special instruction during the entire year; others may only need support for a very localized problem for a short time. The IEP should clearly state the time dimensions involved for each day and for longer periods of time. For the social studies teacher, this is an indefinite component, as the variables are numerous. However, the social studies teacher, in cooperation with others, both inside and outside school, will be able to determine the degree and nature of support. This effort will require teacher planning of class instruction and coordination of support services.

- **Required Periods of Time.** The same variables, as previously described, apply to this component. The impact for social studies teachers is the same. Since the teacher helped to design the IEP, the temporal dimension of the plan will be known.

- **Evaluation of Program Goals.** The purpose of this component is to determine the student's progress in achieving IEP goals. The evaluation plan should be formative. Questions to be asked include: Are we getting there? What, if anything, should be changed? Are we on schedule?

   Modifications are not viewed as defeat or failure, but as positive refinements that will promote success. The key ingredient in this component is the degree to which goals and instructional objectives are stated in behavioral terms. If the statement of student behaviors is specific, then progress can be established and blockages can be identified. This will be a difficult task, as social studies teachers usually operate in generic terms. Considerable practice will be needed to develop skill in stating student behavioral outcomes. To the degree that this is successful, it will positively correlate with the effectiveness of the evaluation component required in an IEP.

- **Due Process.** Interwoven in the design and execution of the IEP is the concept of due process. Students and/or their parents (or surrogates) have the right to review the IEP, monitor its implementation, and have access to legal action, if they believe the system has not worked. This is a two-way sword, for the school and teacher also have the right to due process, to obtain testimony, and to confront witnesses. Students are also encouraged to participate in the construction of their own IEP. Since parents also sign their approval of the IEP, this is a splendid opportunity to involve them in supporting the instructional program designed for their child.

ILLUSTRATIONS

For purposes of illustration, representative samples of both the Individual Educational Program (long term) and the Individual Educational Plan (short term) are provided. These samples reveal a few paths, among the many available to social studies teachers, to take to fulfill this aspect of the law.

1. A team from Massachusetts, Thomas Banit and Eileen Cunningham, have provided the following statement and IEP.[3]

Figure 1 is a partial IEP (Social Studies Section only) for a sophomore student placed in a Team Teaching class. Two pages were combined to better illustrate the relationship between the General Student-Centered Goal and the Specific Student-Centered Objectives.

To fully understand and implement this plan, it is essential that involved staff be aware of, and apply, the information describing the learning style of the student (this would be given prior to the goals on the IEP).

Figure 1. Partial IEP—Social Studies Section—One Semester

Current Performance Level	General Student-Centered Goals	Priority Number	Teaching Approach and Methodology Monitoring and Evaluation Techniques Specialized Equipment and Materials
Has completed a ninth-grade Social Studies class with minimal success. Reading is presently measured at the fourth-grade level, and writing skills are marginal.	Will demonstrate a basic understanding of the social characteristics of the American Nation (Sophomore Curriculum).	3	Team Teaching/ varied groupings and materials/adaptations as needed by resource room staff/point system/informal and formal testing/class grade.

Goal Number	Objective Number	Specific Student-Centered Objectives	Quarters during which objectives will be addressed 1 2 3 4
3	1	Will identify the six categories of culture (economics, family, religion, education, government, and language/art).	X X
3	2	Will describe contemporary American culture based on six characteristics.	X X
3	3	Will identify the sources of American immigrant groups and Black Americans and Native Americans.	X
3	4	Will identify the reasons for immigration to America.	X
3	5	Will identify immigrant settlement locations.	X
3	6	Will describe the experiences of the immigrant crossing.	X
3	7	Will describe the early experiences of the immigrants upon arrival.	X
3	8	Will identify the impact of America on the immigrants.	X
3	9	Will identify the impact of the immigrants on America.	X
3	10	Will compare and contrast recent American immigrants with past groups.	X

3	11	Will identify reasons for existence of racism.	X
3	12	Will actively participate in a small group.	X X
3	13	Will complete Social Studies readings at a mid-fourth grade level.	X X
3	14	Will answer test questions utilizing complete sentences.	X X
3	15	Will answer essay questions by listing major points.	X X
3	16	Will demonstrate auditory attentive ability by completing guide sheets for listening activities.	X X
3	17	Will demonstrate ability to organize work by maintaining a student class folder.	X X
3	18	Will improve note-taking skills by copying outlines from teacher transparancies.	X X
3	19	Will demonstrate ability to utilize charts and graphs.	X X
3	20	Will be able to identify continents and oceans and locate 50% of the American states.	X X
3	21	Will be able to gain meaning and make inferences from Social Studies-related pictures.	X X
3	22	Will be able to construct and draw implications from a time line.	X X
3	23	Will be able to list and describe required Social Studies evidence and data.	X X
3	24	Will draw inferences from 25% of the data and evidence used in class.	X X
3	25	Will identify positive and negative feelings on the social concepts presented.	X X
3	26	Will begin to develop critically a humanistic value system.	X X
3	27	Will demonstrate ability to rationally control her own life and her environment.	X X

Learning Style (current educational status)

June is a strong auditory learner who has not developed adequate reading and writing skills. Past school records indicate that her weaknesses in visual-motor integration contributed heavily to her skill deficiency. Although she has experienced frequent school failure, she is still highly motivated to learn and to achieve a High School Diploma.

June rarely, if ever, participates in a large-group setting. She is very aware of her handicap and will not risk humiliation in front of her peers. She functions best in small, secure groups, where she is assured success.

All reading assignments should be at a fourth-fifth grade level. To increase her skills, teachers should provide vocabulary activities and comprehension questions prior to reading. When possible, June should be allowed opportunities to express her learning through verbal communication (tapes/oral responses). Her cognitive ability is well developed, and required written examinations will not give a true indication of what she has mastered.

2. Thomas Howard and Alan Waidelich, a team from Yorktown Heights High School, Yorktown Heights, New York, have provided the following example of an IEP for a semester-long program. (See Figure 2a, 2b, and 2c.)[4]

Figure 2a. Individualizec

Yorktown Central School District
198 -8   Data

198 -8   Data

Originating
Teacher: _____

IEP Year
Teacher: _____

School: _____

School: _____

Check: Res. Room ☐   Spec. Class ☐   Itin. ☐   Res. Room ☐   Spec. Class ☐   Itin. ☐

MEETING DATA

SPECIAL STRENGTHS
(NOTE: Include comments for both

Spring Meeting, 19   :
Date: _____
Location: _____
Attending: Title or Relation
_____|_____
_____|_____
_____|_____
_____|_____

Early Fall Meeting, 19   :
Date: _____
Location: _____
Attending: Title or Relation
_____|_____
_____|_____
_____|_____
_____|_____

Spring (Final) Meeting, 19   :
Date: _____
Location: _____
Attending: Title or Relation
_____|_____
_____|_____
_____|_____
_____|_____

Recommended Placement for the
Fall: _____
_____
_____

Other student information: _____
_____
_____

Describe extent to which student will be
participating in regular school programs: __

Relevant medical information: _____

(Student's File Copy)

Education Plan for 198 -8

Student's Name: _____
                    Last   First

Home District: _____ Date of Birth ___/___/___
Name of Parent
or Guardian: _____ Home Phone: _____

Home Address: _____

_____ Zip _____

WEAKNESSES	EDUCATIONAL TESTING DATA

Academic and Personal/Social Areas)

EDUCATIONAL TESTING DATA

	Test Name	Score	Date Given
Reading Scores: Incoming	___	___	___
Math Scores: Incoming	___	___	___

Instructional Level of Materials Used
    Incoming (Spring) READING _____
    Incoming (Spring) MATH _____

I.Q. Test Data: Test Name _____
Verbal   Performance   Full Scale
I.Q. _____   I.Q. _____ I.Q. _____
Given By: _____ Date: _____

Retest Data: Test Name _____
Verbal   Performance   Full Scale
I.Q. _____   I.Q. _____ I.Q. _____
Given By: _____ Date: _____

Other Test Data:	Test Name	Score	Date Given
	___	___	___
	___	___	___
	___	___	___
	___	___	___
	___	___	___

Math Scores:	Test	Score	Date
End of Year	___	___	___
Reading Scores: End of Year	___	___	___

Instructional Level of Materials Used
    End of year READING _____
    End of Year MATH _____

Figure 2b. IEP Goal Sheet School Year 19   -19

Yorktown Central School District

Last   (Student Name)   First

Summary of Progress
Toward Each Goal

To be completed for or at
the Spring, 19   Final Meeting.

Goal Number	Date Goal Devel.	Listing of Academic and Personal-Social Goals Established for This School Year	Goal Mastered State "yes" or "no"	Comment

IEP—Page 2

(Use letters of A, B, etc. . . .
if more than one goal sheet is used.)

Figure 2c. IEP Objectives Evaluation Sheet School Year 19   -19

Yorktown Central School District

Last   (Student Name)   First

Instructional Area _____

STATUS REPORT

Show prog. towards each obj. by evaluating continuously & by writing dates in approp. column

Goal Number (see Pg. 2)	Date Obj. Devel.	Conditions— Methods, Materials or Services To Be Used	Short-term Instructional Objectives	Standard or Criteria by Which Mastery of This Objective Will Be Evaluated	Init.	Prog.	Mast.	N/App.

IEP— Page 3

(Use letters of A, B, etc. . . .
if more than one obj.- eval. sheet is used.)

(Student's File Copy)

3. To illustrate a short-term IEP, Marilyn Gross, a resource room teacher from York Central School, Greigsville, New York, provides us with this sample form. (See Figure 3.)[5]

Figure 3

Child _____ Identification # _____

Short Term Goal (s):

Instructional Objective(s)	Current Functioning	Methods or Materials	Dates Beg.	End	Evaluation Procedure and Comments
					Objectives Met
					Yes / No / Still Progressing
					☐ ☐ ☐
					☐ ☐ ☐
					☐ ☐ ☐
					☐ ☐ ☐

4. A social studies teacher and a resource room team, Bradley Stanton, Lynn Erdle, and Mary Ann Bianco, from Canandaigua Academy, Canandaigua, New York, sent us a sample form used in the development of an IEP, part of a course on World Culture. (See Figure 4.)[6]

Figure 4. Resource Room Contact Sheet

Student: Chris S.

Resource Room Teachers: Ms. Bianco and Ms. Erdle

Course: World Cultures   Period: 3rd

Please indicate name of text: _____

*Course Goals:

1. First to learn to think on their own.
2. To accept the fact that ideas that are different or strange are not necessarily wrong with regard to other cultures.
3. To be able to communicate orally without excessive phrases.

Mutually Developed IEP Goals:

1. The student will recognize, spell, and define weekly vocabulary words from social studies lessons.
2. The student will correct and rewrite any written assignments from social studies with assistance from the LD teacher.
3. Chris will practice, on a regular basis, verbally expressing his ideas, from social studies class, in a concise manner.

Specific spelling and/or vocabulary words students will need to know:

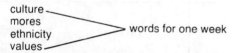

culture
mores
ethnicity
values
> words for one week

Curriculum Modifications/Resources:

Chris' problem is primarily one of being unable to express himself in writing. He will not be successful in class unless he is given the opportunity to express his ideas orally. Consideration might also be given to him to take tests orally.

*Provided by Social Studies teacher, Mr. Stanton.

Conclusion

The numerous elements of an IEP apparently create an additional set of tasks for already overburdened social studies teachers: additional meetings, cooperative arrangements with ancillary personnel, and utilization of additional materials and equipment. However, the components listed in an IEP represent sound teaching and have been found in many classrooms in the past. The major difference is in the degree of specification of objectives, in the materials used, and in the amount of preplanning that heretofore have not been required. Any time spent in preplanning will pay dividends in terms of teacher time and effectiveness. Also these components will force social studies teachers to identify and operationalize long-term and short-term goals. The analysis and synthesis activities involved can only enhance the social studies learning of all students—handicapped or not—in the course and improve the instructional delivery systems of teachers.

Another "fall out" of the IEP is the integration and cooperation that ensue both within and without the school. In both the design and application of the IEP, social studies teachers will come in close working contact with a range of support people, ancillary services, community agencies, and parents. Developing coping behaviors for this new constellation of people and services will require new patterns of survival. The end product of a broader and richer social studies class for children will result. The anxiety about the new will be relieved by the satisfaction of constructing social studies classes that reflect a wider community of people, services, and learning.

Footnotes

[1] Maynard C. Reynolds and Jack W. Birch, *Teaching Exceptional Children in All America's Schools* (Reston, Virginia: The Council for Exceptional Children, 1977), p. 157.

[2] The authors are indebted for the organization of this section on the content of the IEP to Reynolds and Birch, *ibid.*, pp. 159-162.

[3] This statement and IEP were submitted by Thomas Banit and Eileen Cunningham.

[4] This IEP was submitted by Thomas Howard and Alan Waidelich.

[5] This IEP form was submitted by Marilyn Gross.

[6] This referral form was submitted by Bradley Stanton, Lynn Erdle, and Mary Ann Bianco.

"... a variety of other individualized processes prove useful for the mainstreamed student."

5. Modes of Instruction

George P. Gregory

This chapter describes a variety of instructional modes which the regular classroom teacher can employ in teaching and working with mainstreamed students. In an attempt to build on earlier chapters, the suggestions which follow assume a team approach to mainstreaming, with parents, administrators, classroom teachers, and special teachers working together as they determine what to teach and how to teach it. In planning instructional strategies appropriate for students enrolled in mainstreamed classes, no one strategy represents the most effective mode of instruction. Rather, experts recommend a varied approach based upon the learning styles and rates, previous experiences, and knowledge of students. Teachers should therefore view the instructional strategies which follow in this light and design their own units of instruction by drawing from combinations of these strategies.

Mainstreaming Strategies for the Social Studies

A variety of instructional strategies exists for teachers interested in the integration of handicapped students into regular classes. Figure 1 displays five of these strategies and lists implications for each strategy in terms of their effects on the regular classroom teacher.[1]

Figure 1. Mainstreaming Strategies for Social Studies

Strategy	Implications for the Classroom Teacher				
	Changes in Curricular Offerings —Topics—Content	Revisions of Student Materials	Development of New Materials	Revision of Teaching Strategies	Changes in Evaluation Procedures
1. Rewrite the Book	NO	YES	MAYBE	MAYBE	MAYBE
2. Grouping	NO	YES	YES	YES	YES
3. New Courses	YES	YES	YES	YES	YES
4. Worksheet Approach	NO	YES	MAYBE	NO	MAYBE
5. Individualize	YES/NO	YES	YES	YES	YES

Question: 1. Which strategy requires the most change?
2. Which strategy requires the least change?
3. Which strategy best provides for individual needs, interests, and concerns?

G. Gregory, 1977

• **Rewrite the Book.** One strategy which a teacher might employ involves rewriting classroom materials to fit the reading level(s) of mainstreamed students. With the assistance of the reading and special education teacher, the regular social studies teacher would adapt, rewrite, and edit parts of textbooks and other instructional materials to fit reading and interest levels of handicapped students. If a social studies teacher adopts this approach, it will not require changing curricular offerings and topics, but will result in revision of student materials, the design of new materials, and modification of teaching strategies and evaluation techniques.

• **Grouping.** In addition to rewriting textbook materials, teachers can also group mainstreamed and regular students to provide more effective instruction. To accomplish this task, teachers might use sociograms, information about student strengths and weaknesses in specific skill areas (e.g., reading, map skills, chart and graph interpretation), and peer tutoring.
    As Lowenbraun and Affleck note, three possible grouping arrangements exist for the social studies teacher. Students can be grouped in "skill-specific"groups which work on a specific learning task.[2] For example, when the class works on map-reading skills the teacher might group together those students who need instruction in specific subset map-reading areas. One group might focus on cardinal directions, another on map scale, a third on simple map interpretation (community and school maps), and a fourth group on more advanced map reading and analysis (state and national maps). By determining specific map-skill levels, teachers could then assign mainstreamed and regular students to appropriate groups.[3]

Another grouping arrangement calls for homogenous groups comprised of students operating at similar levels of ability. For example, if the entire class is completing an assignment or project dealing with the American Revolution, the teacher might form ability groups based upon observation of all skill areas. Each group would study the same topic but use evidence packs containing materials of varying complexity.

A third grouping strategy involves heterogenous arrangements. Lowenbraun and Affleck suggest placing mainstreamed students in groups having a range of skills and gearing individual assignments to meet student needs. For example, after a heterogenous group reads a passage from a textbook, the teacher might ask questions having different comprehension focuses: recall or detail, sequencing, main idea, critical analysis, and creative thinking.

> After reading a portion of the selection, the teacher might ask each child a specific question geared at his or her level of comprehension: "John, how many boys are in the story?"; "Sue, where did the boys go after they finished their lunch?"; "Charles, what would be a good title for the story?"; "Fred, do you think this story could actually have taken place?"; "Mark, how might you have solved the boys' problem?"[4]

Peer tutoring represents another grouping strategy closely linked to heterogenous groups. As Mara Sapon-Shevin notes, peer tutors can assist less able students to gain proficiency in social studies skill areas.[5] For example, one effective pairing might involve placing a student who is at the stage of initial acquisition of a skill with a student who has gained proficiency in that skill. One student might be able to interpret a chart or graph while a mainstreaming student might need assistance in identifying the elements of a graph or chart. By pairing these two students with a structured chart or graph reading task, both students benefit.[6]

A number of techniques exist for initiating peer teaching for social studies instruction. The teacher might design a peer teaching directory which contains the strengths of individual students. Students might interview each other to determine who is good at what skills.[7] Students needing assistance could then consult the directory to identify a peer tutor. Once tutors are identified, the teacher might then conduct peer teaching training sessions to assist peer tutors in working with mainstreamed and handicapped students. Experienced peer teachers, teachers, school administrators, counselors, and ancillary personnel might help facilitate these sessions.[8] Once trained, tutors can assist in completing reading assignments, summarizing textbook chapters, tape-recording difficult reading passages, and designing learning activities for less able students.[9]

As Figure 1 indicates, grouping strategies will not require changes in topics or course content. However, social studies teachers will need to revise student materials (e.g., study guides, group tasks, group study sheets), develop new materials, and revise teaching strategies and evaluation procedures.

• **New Courses.** A third mainstreaming strategy for the social studies involves designing new courses or units of instruction. A review of social studies curriculum guides for mildly handicapped students indicates a wide variety of functional, practical topics. For example, many guides suggest focusing on the immediate environments of the home, school, and community throughout the K-12 social studies program. Most primary (K-3) social studies programs for mildly handicapped students include study about the self, family, school, and immediate neighborhood. At the intermediate level, students in early programs learn about their state and American History, and begin investigating possible vocational choices. Junior and senior high school programs concentrate on pre-vocational, survival, and consumer-related skills. Few curricula suggest teaching about other cultures or employing a social sciences approach to studying these cultures.[10]

In designing new courses or units of instruction for mainstreaming classes, the teacher needs to integrate those social studies topics taught in special education classes into the existing social studies program. For example, by identifying those social studies topics taught at the junior high level in special education classes, the teacher can design new instructional units which include some of these topics and fit them into the existing program. Turnbull and Schulz suggest the following questions when considering the kinds of social studies topics appropriate for mainstreamed students:

> 1. Will these topics help the student become more independent in the community, employment setting, and/or at home?
> 2. What is the jeopardy of the student not knowing this information or being able to master this skill?
> 3. Will the student be receiving this information from other sources?[11]

Responses to these questions and a review of special education programs will help to match student needs and interests to the long-range goals of the social studies program.

As displayed in Figure 1, designing new courses will require the greatest amount of modification by the social studies teacher. In addition to changing course content, teachers would need to revise student materials, develop new materials, revise teaching strategies, and modify evaluation techniques.

• **Worksheet Approach.** A fourth mainstreaming strategy for the social studies involves the use of study guides and worksheets to accompany textbooks used by students. Worksheets can facilitate instruction in reading and basic social studies skills. When designed to fit the entry level skills of mainstreamed students, study guides can help these students keep pace with the rest of the class.

Lowenbraun and Affleck have identified several guidelines for designing worksheets and study guides:

> 1. Use simple, clearly written directions. Ask perception-checking questions which require mainstreamed students to restate instructions in their own words.

2. Use one specific task per worksheet page or assignment.

3. Employ one format for worksheets so that the mainstreamed students can easily recognize assignments.

4. Be sure that the mainstreamed student understands the exact demands of the task and when he or she has completed that task.

5. Insure success on student-directed tasks by using visual and verbal prompts.[12]

A second type of worksheet approach calls for the use of learning activity packets (LAPS) or evidence packets to supplement textbook content. LAPS can assist mainstreamed students in learning one basic concept or idea which has been broken down into several components.[13] The following map-reading LAP serves as an example of a format which might be used in designing packets to accompany textbook content.

Read a Map. Level Intermediate.

Objectives: Student will read a simple classroom map by:
    a. identifying the elements of the map
    b. pointing to various objects which appear on the map
    c. describing how to locate various objects or learning
       centers in the classroom
Pretest: Ask student to interpret and read a classroom map.

Activities:
    Follow task analysis of map reading. Given a simple
    classroom map, student will:
    a. name all of the objects shown
    b. point to all objects in the room which are displayed on the map
    c. walk from one object or place to another
    d. locate the social studies learning center on the map
       and in the classroom

Branching Activities:
    a. Given a map of the school, student locates specific
       areas and moves from one location to another
    b. Given a map of the community, student locates points of
       interest and describes how to get to them
    c. Student maps home or apartment

• **Individualize.** The fifth mainstreaming strategy listed on Figure 1, individualization, is closely allied to both the grouping and worksheet approaches. Individualization requires that the teacher use achievement test scores, the mainstreamed student's IEP, and other pertinent diagnostic data to determine topics, instructional materials, and evaluation techniques. Ideally, each mainstreamed student would receive a social studies individualized program which defines long-term goals, materials, and evaluation instruments. This program would utilize content from the specified grade level and assist the mainstreamed student's integration into the regular classroom.

One critical element in preparing individualized programs for mainstreamed students involves task analysis. Task analysis requires breaking each task into its component parts and then sequencing these parts into a developmental arrangement. For example, before students can learn to read maps, they must understand the following concepts: up-down; near-far; smaller than-larger than; left-right; north-south-east-west; and the concept of scale. By designing map-reading activities which include instruction about these concepts, the teacher can determine which students need further instruction and which students can work with more complex map-reading materials.

Turnbull and Schulz suggest the following strategy in preparing task-analyzed activities.

> To analyze a learning task, first state the terminal objective, which tells what the learner will be able to do after instruction. To analyze the overall task, ask questions like: What must the learner be able to do to achieve the objective? What kinds of learning are involved? What prior skills are necessary? What specific knowledge is required? What concepts or meanings must be understood? What is prerequisite to ultimate success?[14]

In addition to task-analyzed instruction, a variety of other individualized processes prove useful for the mainstreamed student. Peer teaching, learning centers, contracts, and learning activity packets represent examples of such strategies. Peer teaching and learning activity packets were discussed earlier.

Learning centers and learning stations provide an area of the class-room where students can independently complete social studies activities. These centers can focus on basic social studies skills, the acquisition of new concepts or topics, or the reinforcement of social studies instruction. The following steps serve as a guide in designing learning centers for the mainstreamed social studies classroom:

> 1. Select the skill or concept to be taught, reinforced, or enriched.
> 2. Develop the skill or concept into a series of learning activities which include manipulation, experimentation, listening, and/or viewing.
> 3. Prepare the skill or concept into an application activity: filling in; sequencing; putting together; taking apart; listening; checking; classifying; matching; tracing; writing; and/or labeling.
> 4. Incorporate the skill or concept into an extending activity: developing your own map; researching your family tree; constructing a colonial village; predicting an outcome.
> 5. Place all the games, worksheets, charts, and materials together in one area of the room for all students to use in self-instruction.[15]

Learning contracts also offer mainstreamed students opportunities to work independently on social studies content. A contract between the student and teacher includes a definition of the topic or problem, behavioral objectives, a listing of possible learning resources, and a series of learning activities that provide the student with choices in gathering, organizing, classifying, and reporting information.[16] Since contracts enable mainstreamed students to work at their own pace and with materials suited to their needs, they offer a useful alternative for individualized instruction.

Conclusion

A number of instructional techniques exist for social studies teachers involved in mainstreaming. These strategies range from rewriting student materials to complete individualization of instruction. As displayed in Figure 1, each technique involves specific implications for the teacher. As teachers plan for mainstreamed students, they will need to match their own teaching styles to those strategies which best meet the needs of these students. For example, if a teacher currently employs a wide variety of instructional materials, she or he might decide to group students for social studies instruction. By the teacher providing each group with study guides, all students can gather information and contribute to full class presentations. If teachers utilize one textbook for social studies, they might want to rewrite parts of that book and provide individualized tasks for mainstreamed students. Such individualization would help these students to take part in full class activities and to share their information with other class members. In other cases, teachers might decide to design new units of instruction or full-semester social studies courses which better fit the needs and interests of both regular and mainstreamed students.

The curriculum model presented in Figure 1 synthesizes one approach to mainstreaming in the social studies classroom. This approach focuses on teaching strategies and instructional materials, since these two components of teaching and learning will most directly affect the mainstreamed student. As teachers prepare to work with these students, they might use this model to evaluate their own instructional techniques and design lessons and activities which provide effective learning experiences for all students.

Footnotes

[1]George Gregory, "Using the Newspaper in the Mainstreamed Classroom,"*Social Education* 43 (February 1979): 140.

[2]Sheila Lowenbraun and James Q. Affleck, *Teaching Mildly Handicapped Children in Regular Classes* (Columbus, Ohio: Charles E. Merrill, 1976), pp.94-5.

[3]See: Barbara Christesen, *Map Skills A, B, C, D* (Scholastic Magazine, 1978) for task-analysed student materials focusing on reading and interpreting maps and globes.

[4]Lowenbraun and Affleck, *op. cit.*, pp. 94-5.

[5]Mara Sapon-Shevin, "Another Look at Mainstreaming: Exceptionality, Normality, and the Nature of Difference," *Phi Delta Kappan* 60 (October 1978): 119-121.

[6]Lowenbraun and Affleck, *op. cit.*, p. 97.

[7]Ann P. Turnbull and Jane B Schulz, *Mainstreaming Handicapped Students: A Guide for the Classroom Teacher* (Copyright © 1979 by Allyn and Bacon, Inc., Boston. Reprinted with permission). pp. 109-110.

[8]*Ibid.*, pp. 111-112.

[9]*Ibid.*, p. 266.

[10]See: ERIC files for following curriculum guides: ED 091 902 (Escambia County, Florida); ED 036 012 (Charlotte-Mecklenburg, North Carolina); ED 046 809 (Los Angeles City Schools, California); and ED 030 999 (Ohio State Department of Education)—which list suggested topics and programs for mildly handicapped students.

[11]Turnbull and Schulz, *op. cit.*, p. 260.

[12]Lowenbraun and Affleck, *op. cit.*, p.63.

[13]Turnbull and Schulz, *op. cit.*, pp. 116-117.

[14]S.R. Johnson and R.B. Johnson, *Developing Individualized Instructional Material* (Palo Alto, California: Westinghouse Learning Press, 1970). Cited in Turnbull and Schulz, *op. cit.*, p. 95.

[15]Turnbull and Schulz, *op. cit.*, pp. 113-114.

[16]*Ibid.*, pp. 115.

"Numerous change-of-pace activities related to teaching social studies concepts must be considered. . . ."

6.Organizing and Presenting Social Studies Content in a Mainstreamed Class

Howard Sanford

The purpose of this chapter is to offer social studies teachers a number of suggestions as to techniques/strategies they might employ with a variety of handicapped students to ensure a successful mainstreaming situation for all students involved—handicapped and non-handicapped.

General Suggestions

The following are a few general suggestions for the regular classroom teacher to meet the needs of handicapped students in the classroom.

• Promote individualization of instruction by utilizing a variety of materials, different assignments, and different groupings.

• Many non-handicapped students in a regular classroom may have minor learning problems in the retention/comprehension of social studies content. If material or a strategy has worked with these youngsters, it may be employed with some handicapped students after an initial trial period.

• The handicapped are not a homogeneous group, but are more like the non-handicapped in terms of their heterogeneity. All have varying strengths, weaknesses, interests, and needs. Different handicapping conditions will require different instructional strategies.

  a. Learning disabled students will require a review of previously introduced social studies content, as well as a number of opportunities to apply the content. Perhaps different instructional materials will be needed to introduce, teach, or reinforce a particular concept.
  b. Mildly retarded students may require a reduced scope or different emphasis of the curriculum, at least initially. Infusion of, or integration of, functional daily living and vocationally related skills/activities with the regular social studies class curriculum may be appropriate.
  c. Auditorily impaired, visually impaired, and physically handicapped pupils may require special mate-

rials, seating, equipment, illumination devices, increased volume, listening tapes of the social studies text, raised maps, special lighting, special paper and pencils, or the use of a typewriter.

It should be noted that handicapped individuals within each of the preceding groups may have different individual learning styles, rates, memory/application levels, motivational/reinforcement requirements, and individual reading, listening, and comprehension levels as they apply to the social studies.

• Since the regular classroom teacher cannot be expected to generate a one-to-one situation for each handicapped student in the room, consideration must be given to a variety of group activities or project work (individual, small group, class), as well as to the use of a variety of instructional materials. Group activities have a particular relationship to the area of social studies and should be considered as appropriate instructional strategies. These measures must be modified for use with individual handicapped students as well as non-handicapped students.

• The social studies teacher will have access to and information on a number of instructional resources from special education and the cooperation of/coordination with the special education resource room teacher on a daily basis for learning disabled and mentally handicapped students. The regular classroom teacher can also expect the assistance of a special education itinerant teacher to provide the specialized materials and equipment needed for specialized cases, such as visually and auditorily impaired students.

Planning Appropriate Curriculum

However, the most important aspect of providing a successful mainstreaming experience for each handicapped child may be the analysis of the present social studies curriculum/course of study. Decisions as to what to teach, what to emphasize, and in what sequence must be established before decisions as to with what (materials), with whom (groups, other teachers), and where (placement) are made. This whole process, while an essential feature of IEP development for handicapped students, should be a major concern for all teachers in terms of planning and carrying out instruction for all students. A lack of specificity, of relevance, of concerns, and of goals is found in some social studies curricula. Also the emphasis on memorizing information and facts, as opposed to teaching concepts, understandings, generalizations, and skills, is a deterrent to a successful instructional program in social studies for all students, especially the handicapped.

One technique that should be considered by the classroom teacher for use with handicapped children in a regular class setting is the essential content checklist. Since many curricula or curricula guides used in regular class settings contain objectives that are general, the teachers must have access to a system that will enable them to have broad content areas or topics broken down into sequential component topics or tasks.

The questions of what to teach and in what sequence are especially important for handicapped students in a mainstreamed setting. The scope and sequence of a social studies curriculum or course may contain a number of concepts or information sets that are not a functional part of student skills. If curricular design is not organized in sequential learning steps that lead to concept formation or development, there will be major content gaps that contribute to failure experiences for both handicapped and non-handicapped.

The successful integration of handicapped students with regular class curricula can be greatly aided by examining the term "specially designed instruction" as mandated by P.L. 94-142. Three key concepts must be kept in mind when planning appropriate instruction for handicapped students in a regular class setting.

> 1. Some handicapped students will be able to handle the same curricular content as the non-handicapped students, with specialized materials/arrangements. For instance, visually handicapped students have access to illumination/magnification devices to read standard texts and texts with enlarged type, as well as the use of tactile devices, such as specially developed relief maps. The auditorily handicapped have available to them amplification of sound devices, or special seating, or hearing aids.
>
> 2. Many handicapped students and non-handicapped students will learn the same course content and be more motivated to learn if the content is presented in a manner, or through material, that indicates a more relevant or integrated relationship to standard course content. For example, the development of concepts, as a central core of the social studies curriculum, can be effected with an emphasis on project work of thematic learning centers.
>
> 3. A number of handicapped students (mildly mentally handicapped and some learning disabled students) may benefit from a prioritization of the standard social studies content at a particular level that may involve the modification of some course content for some individuals.

Content checklists, as an instructional tool with handicapped persons, evolved due to the lack of appropriate, comprehensive, sequential curricula and/or the ambiguity contained in many curricula guides. The content checklist format, which is made up of broad subject or skill areas broken down into specific subcomponents and placed into a sequence using a task-analysis procedure, has a number of advantages for a teacher working with handicapped students.

1. It is an aid in the development and monitoring of an Individualized Educational Plan (IEP) through the specification of skill sequences and student progress through the sequence.

2. It provides the basis for the development of criteria-referenced tests which are an essential feature of the IEP process, but it also enables the teacher to analyze, prioritize, plan for, and teach specific skills, concepts, or information.

3. By a teacher taking a checklist and writing the objectives in behavioral terms, the checklist can be an effective means to report progress to parents, as well as a useful tool in reporting important student information to other teachers working with that student (resource room teacher, special teacher, regular class teacher).

However, many curricula guides and content sequences in the area of social studies (and other subjects) contain requirements that are either too abstract, or utilize skill requirements for which the student does not possess the conceptual or factual background/prerequisites. The assumption that any student (handicapped or non-handicapped) is ready to learn some component of the course content because other students in the same class are ready, or because that information falls in the next chapter or page in a text or workbook, is not valid. It would seem that necessary components of a skill-development hierarchy in the social studies would include:

• access to skill hierarchies/sequences for the different content areas within the social studies curriculum from basic information and facts, extending through related concepts and generalizations, and ending with specific skills to be attained by this sequence.

• identification of which facts, concepts, generalizations, and skills the individual already possesses.

The actual development and make-up of an essential content checklist designed for a skills hierarchical schema depend on several content decisions. These would include:

1. The identification and teaching of prerequisite facts, concepts, and generalizations. It can be assumed that many mildly mentally handicapped and learning disabled students will lack certain prerequisites to the social studies content that the rest of the class has acquired. In order to develop an understanding of social studies content, these prerequisites must be identified, sequenced, and taught both separately (by individual studywork, learning centers, the resource room teacher) and integrated with the regular classwork whenever possible.

2. The identification of those facts, concepts, generalizations, and skills that are essential to each lesson/unit. Some handicapped students may never achieve all of these goals due to the nature of their learning problems. Therefore, the social studies teacher must set priorities for these content goals in terms of integration, coordination, and concept building. The instructor must make decisions concerning repetition, emphasis, modification, or alternative information and learning exercises for segments of each lesson/unit of the course.

3. The planning of appropriate social studies goals and objectives for a handicapped child. The teacher must identify alternative ways that a concept or generalization may be stated and presented. The content for a particular social studies topic could be sequenced along a schema like Bloom's Taxonomic Structure. The sequence of objectives extends from complex thinking skills (high level) to basic memorizations skills (low level). Each level has a number of different ways the skills may be identified, taught, or demonstrated; e.g., evaluation—comparing, contrasting, and judging; knowledge—copying, identifying, and labeling. Therefore, different learning activities, at the same cognitive level, can be conducted in order to provide an appropriate learning modality for each student.

Presenting Social Studies in a Mainstreamed Class

The other major aspect of this chapter deals with presenting social studies education in a mainstreamed class. The range and degree of learning problems—academic, emotional, physical—prohibit the setting down of specific "do's and don'ts." The following methodological and procedural guidelines should be considered in organizing instructional time:

• Many handicapped students learn at a much slower rate.

• Some handicapped pupils require overlearning of concepts through a variety of activities.

• Many visually and auditorily impaired students are easily fatigued due to the great deal of concentration and effort that is required to use Braille equipment, to use special paper/pencils, and to use illumination, magnification, and amplification devices. Also, the hearing-impaired students must expend great concentration and effort to use speech-reading techniques to "hear" the teacher.

• A number of handicapped students may exhibit a short attention span, memory problems, language problems, and behavior problems. If the lecture/discussion method of teaching social studies concepts is overused, many of these behaviors will increase/be reinforced, and prevent learning. Some children with behavioral emotional difficulties might be more successful in small-group discussions for short time periods than in large-group discussions for longer periods.

• Numerous change-of-pace activities related to teaching social studies concepts must be considered by the classroom teacher. These could include projects (individual, group, class); using media; and learning-interest-exploratory centers (listening station; interest reading-history comics; science experiments that relate to learning social studies geographic, climatic, or environmental concepts). Physical disabilities should be considered when assigning projects so that students are given the alternatives to construct, to draw, to tape record a story, or to do other activities.

• Many handicapped students of all types may exhibit memory problems, especially related to the specific vocabulary of social studies. The teacher should emphasize key points through outlining activities, making use of who-what-when-where-why types of excercises, developing dictionary skills and location of information skills, and compiling picture vocabulary and word files.

• Specific teacher questions and related activities which call for student responses of a higher cognitive level beyond recall/memorization can lead to extended attention span and an increased retention of information through a variety of uses/applications. These efforts can make social studies content more relevant by developing those skills that are related to problem solving and decision making. Some children who have difficulty learning from printed material can be successful in discussions on questions of values.

• Media, pictures, charts, films, and filmstrips can provide the variety of instruction that lends itself to overlearning/application/retention of a concept. However, many visually impaired cannot profit from many traditional media forms and activities without adapted materials. A number of geographic aids—including Braille atlases; relief maps of a molded plastic texture; dissected and undissected maps of continents and countries; relief globes and mileage scales; large type outline maps; and land-form models featuring three-dimensional tactile maps which illustrate and teach geographic concepts—are available. Several sources of these adaptive materials and others like "talking books" and taped versions are found in Chapter 11, "Representative Resources."

• The hearing-impaired students in the social studies class may require or need special seating, skill in speech reading, awareness on the teacher's part to articulate his/her speech and/or to speak more slowly, and a listening helper. It is also suggested that the teacher place specific social studies vocabulary terms on the board or on a well illuminated screen or surface (overhead transparency). Proper care of the student's hearing aid may also correlate with the amount of learning which takes place. A very important type of media for hearing-impaired students is the use of captioned films and filmstrips. Many of these films and filmstrips may be obtained on a free loan basis. (For sources, see Chapter 11, "Representative Resources.")

• The task of finding and ordering the specialized materials and equipment that visually-impaired and auditorily-impaired students need should not fall primarily on the shoulders of the regular class teacher. It should be provided for by the itinerant or resource room teacher working through the school's committee for the handicapped and in coordination with the social studies teacher.

• One of the major problems of handicapped students, regardless of the type/condition, and of many non-handicapped students is reading deficiency. Social studies texts that are written on a level that is too difficult for the student will lead to continued failure. Different types of reading tasks in the social studies require different types of reading materials. Thus:

a. Different social studies texts with varying reading levels can be employed.

b. Illustrated supplemental texts are useful. (Globe American History comics, Pendulum Press—Illustrated American History.)

c. It is possible to acquire multi-level editions of the same texts.

d. Newspapers and magazines can be included in interest centers.

e. Taped editions of the class text can be used at listening stations.

f. Projects (individual, group, or class) where the students focus on the key vocabulary, illustrations, maps, charts, and summary concepts of a reading selection/chapter are effective.

g. Activities which focus on the functional use of reading materials are beneficial. Locating information, by using the index, table of contents, the dictionary, atlas, and library card catalog, is of value. Reading exercises that develop study skills are also legitimate, appropriate, and potentially motivating activities which can be used with handicapped students in social studies. Some examples would include: outlining (who-what-where-why), identifying topic sentences, skim reading, paraphrasing, creating captions for chapter illustrations, and learning map vocabulary and the vocabulary of charts and graphs.

h. Interest centers for independent reading should be set up where students can read a variety of materials that are written at the student's independent reading levels and that also relate to the social studies content. Information on the student's independent, instructional, listening, comprehension, and interest levels can be obtained from the resource room and/or itinerant teacher.

• The factor of "active learning" or the process of learning by doing implies the integration of subject matter content. The application of subject content to real world materials, problems, and decisions has tremendous significance for meeting the instructional needs of most handicapped students in a mainstreamed social studies program. However, this type of learning seems to relate mainly to the needs of those students who have "learning problems."

Research has generally indicated that there is no simple right method for classroom teachers to use with students who have learning problems. Generally, they may be expected to have language and reading problems, to have trouble remembering content and deriving generalizations, to show frustration and to possess a low self-concept due to continued academic failure, and to exhibit a short attention span and general lack of motivation. Again, recent research has generally indicated that how subject content is presented to students with learning problems, as well as the type of material used, is a very important determinant in how much and how soon content is learned, and whether or not it is retained.

A number of instructional suggestions have been presented for classroom use with students who have learning problems. Alone and in combination with other strategies/techniques, they can be key aids in developing achievement, interest, and motivation in content acquisition and retention with handicapped persons. They are factors that generate conditions of success that lead to further student development and gains.

"Students work individually . . . and at their own pace."

7. Ideas from the Field

The design of this chapter is to present applications of mainstreaming from practitioners in the field—with an emphasis on classroom teachers. The editors solicited manuscripts written by teachers describing the processes and systems they use to implement mainstreaming. A parallel effort was made to secure units and/or lesson plans that would reflect classroom operations in mainstreamed social studies classes. This chapter and Chapter 4 on IEPs were designed to highlight practitioners and their products as used in the field.

Many contributions were received, but space limitations prevented the use of all the manuscripts, units, and lessons submitted. The following selections reflect geographic distribution, variety of handicapping conditions, and a range of grade levels, Many useful contributions are only briefly included in a descriptive section of this chapter, or are represented in a synthesis of all the contributions that appears in the last part of this chapter. The creativity and originality of all who responded reflect the high standards of social studies educators, K-12, and their dedication and commitment to the improvement of instruction.

Contributors to This Chapter:

Thomas F. Banit
Social Studies Teacher
Walpole High School
Walpole, Massachusetts

Eileen J. Cunningham
Program Coordinator, Special Needs
Sudbury Public Schools
Sudbury, Massachusetts

Linda Biemer
Assistant Professor
of Professional Education
SUNY Binghamton
Binghamton, New York

Ronald Pierce
Social Studies Teacher

Gail Abraham
Social Studies Teacher

African Road Junior High School, Vestal, New York

Tee Billingsley
Project Director
"Each One All Together"
Williamson County Schools
Hillsboro Elementary School
Franklin, Tennessee

Thomas F. Howard
Social Studies Teacher

Alan Waidelich
Resource Room Teacher

Yorktown Heights High School, Yorktown Heights, New York

Charles Meisgeier
Professor of Education
University of Houston
Director, Houston Child Service
Demonstration Center
Houston, Texas

Michele M. Paoletti
Elementary Teacher
Woodhaven Schools, Inc.
Columbia, Missouri

Team Teaching
A Practical Application for Mainstreaming

Thomas F. Banit and Eileen J. Cunningham

An adequate and appropriate program is an essential right of all children and one specifically mandated for the special needs population. Individual Educational Plans (IEP) describe learning styles; list current performance levels; establish student-centered goals and objectives; state teaching approaches, methodologies, and evaluation techniques; and note specialized equipment and materials. To implement effectively the IEP of the secondary student, a Team Teaching Model (Social Studies Teacher/Resource Room Teacher) is valuable.

Handicapped children who receive specialized instruction outside of the regular program still spend considerable time in classes that are not designed to meet their special needs. Consultation and support services are usually available, but extremely difficult to deliver in a high school setting, where faculty size, curriculum demands, and student mobility present barriers to communication. Complicating this process is the general lack of classroom teaching experience of the Resource Room staff. Frequently, it is responsible for the development and implementation of the IEP that directly affects the regular educational program, which is the specialty of the content-area teacher. Team Teaching, on a daily basis, allows for a cross-training experience, and opportunity for all students to benefit from different teaching philosophies and from a positive environment for specialized instruction.

The Team Teaching approach requires strong administrative support. Sufficient mutual-planning periods must be built into each teacher's schedule, and students must be carefully placed to construct a well-balanced classroom. Seventy-five percent of these students should be academically motivated with minimal emotional and instructional needs. The remaining twenty-five percent would include students who require significant curriculum adaptations as defined in IEPs and who will receive these services through a Team Teaching Class, specifically stated in the educational plan.

Structuring the classroom to provide the most effective program is a shared responsibility of both the Social Studies Teacher and the Resource Room Teacher in our program. An ongoing priority is the development of a role description for each teacher. This takes considerable time and should not be predetermined by administrators or involved staff. A minimum of six months should be allowed to complete this task, and then it should be constantly reviewed and updated by the people directly involved.

In developing role descriptions, it is important to capitalize on each other's teaching strengths. Students should view both teachers as professionals who are accountable for their education. The Resource Room Teacher should not be identified with only those students with IEPs (and, by inference, who are handicapped). This means that both teachers teach all students in various groupings, share discipline decisions, and agree on final grades. What is taught remains the responsibility of the Social Studies Teacher, but approaches to learning are developed as a team.

Many Special Needs students require highly individualized programs and adapted grade systems. In this Team Teaching Model, every student was provided a folder that contained various activities (teacher-made and commercial), and this was kept within the classroom until needed for a quiz review. A point system was constructed to allow for various abilities and to supply immediate positive reinforcement. All activities were assigned a point value (average 20 points), and these would accumulate over a week's time (maximum week and a half) to 100 points, equal to a quiz grade. In this way, all students had an opportunity to achieve grades commensurate with their efforts and abilities.

A multi-sensory approach to learning was developed for all new concepts. Tapes were used with guide sheets; films and video tapes were incorporated into the curriculum; and picture studies, poetry, role playing, and art projects became meaningful vehicles for learning. Materials, written at various grade levels, were available, and these provided reading activities designed to improve vocabulary and comprehension skills. Students were encouraged to write at their levels and to increase written production, but they were not penalized for poorly developed skills. Word-find puzzles, crosswords, and manipulatives were also constructed to further a total learning experience.

Instruction was provided in standard lecture format, small groups, paired situations, and through individual teaching. During class lectures, students were required to take notes, but this was structured through the use of guide sheets, accompanied by transparencies. Small-group sessons could involve two, three, or four clusters, depending on the objective of the lesson. Most group activities were designed to be completed in one teaching block, although some allowed for one shift in groupings. This was found to be the maximum change possible to ensure continuity and classroom management.

The Team Teaching Model is an effective mechanism for providing the "least restrictive environment" with daily supportive services. Not only does it provide a healthy atmosphere for learning, but it also ensures a valid mainstreaming experience.[1]

Culture Borrowing Lesson Plan
With Adaptations for Use with Hearing-Impaired Students

Michele M. Paoletti

I. Concept: Culture Borrowing

II. Level: Intermediate

III. Introduction — Transitional

"Last week we finished our unit on three fairly isolated cultures. Today we are going to look at what happens when cultures make contact with each other."

IV. Objectives:

A. At the end of the lesson, the students will be able to identify the culture origin of three commonplace substances; e.g., glass, coffee, cotton.

B. After experiencing this lesson on culture borrowing, students will be able to identify, verbally or in written form, three aspects of their lives that have been directly influenced by other cultures.

C. At the end of this lesson, students will be able to speculate on possible ways the above aspects found their way into our culture.

V. Procedure — Closed Induction Strategy

A. Teacher presents examples and non-examples, in which criterial attributes of the concept are embedded, but does not identify them.

1. Teacher presents a display to the class of the following items: calendar, drinking glass, cotton shirt, loose tea, coffee beans, paper, telephone, light bulb (using real objects, not pictures).

B. Students analyze examples and identify (induce) elements the examples have in common (criterial attributes).

1. Teacher asks students to determine what all the items do/do not have in common; then asks them to consider the origin of the items.

C. Students group examples according to criterial attributes.

1. Students put the calendar, drinking glass, shirt, tea, coffee, and paper in one group; they put the light bulb and telephone in another group.

D. Students label groups.

1. Students label the first group of items: "BORROWED FROM OTHER CULTURES"; and label the second group as "FROM OUR CULTURE."

2. Teacher shows on a map the place of origin of the borrowed items.

E. Students generate additional examples and non-examples.

1. Students identify items (aspects) from their own life-styles that have been borrowed from other cultures (e.g., pizza, chow mein, Beatles music).

VI. Evaluation

A. Teacher asks the following questions:

1. What is there in your own daily life that has been borrowed from another culture?

2. Can you identify the cultural origins of glass, cotton, and coffee?
3. How do you think some of these items found their way into our culture?
   B. Mapwork
   Given a list of "borrowed items" and a symbol for each item, and a mimeographed copy of a world map with countries delineated, the student will draw the symbol of the "borrowed item" on the map in the country of its origin.
VII. Closure
   A. There will be a brief review of the items used in day-to-day life that have been borrowed from other cultures.
   B. There will be a brief discussion of ways in which these items found their way into our culture

Adaptations:
   A. When Speaking to the Class:
      1. Speak in a voice that is natural in pace and volume. Do not over-enunciate words; this complicates lipreading.
      2. Always face the class when speaking. Do not speak while writing on the board or pointing out things on the map.
      3. Do not pace while speaking to the class; this complicates lipreading also.
      4. Repeat all questions asked by other class members.
   B. Visual Aids
      1. It is helpful to list key words on the board. For example, in the above lesson, it would be helpful to list the borrowed items and their countries of origin on the board after showing them on the map.
      2. Provide a script or outline of unsubtitled filmstrips or movies to hearing-impaired students. They can derive much more meaning from these visual aids if they know the context or subject matter to be covered.
   C. Group Work
      1. Since receiving information while in a group is more difficult for hearing-impaired students than if this occurred when they were interacting with someone on a one-to-one basis, keep the groups small. This adaptation applies to the Procedure steps B through E in the above lesson plan.
   D. General
      1. Consult with hearing-impaired students periodically to make sure that the adaptations are adequate and that the students are getting all the necessary information.
      2. Don't make it obvious to the whole class that you are making adaptations for your hearing-impaired students. Your subtlety and tact in this area will do much to help the student feel more comfortable and part of the class.
   E. Delivery Systems
      1. Itinerant teachers of the hearing impaired
      2. Resource Room and Resource Teachers
      3. Preplanning with ancillary team and generation of IEP, and timetable of support materials and services throughout year.[2]

United States Constitution

Linda Biemer, Gail Abraham, and Ronald Pierce

Topic: U.S. Constitution   Time: Fifteen (15) class periods

Objectives: Students will be able to

(1) explain why many Americans felt that a new constitution was needed in 1787;
(2) explain how the new constitution was written;
(3) explain the terms "compromise," "separation of powers," "checks and balances," and "judicial review";
(4) explain the process by which a bill introduced into Congress becomes a law;
(5) explain the rationale for an amending process, describe the amending process, and explain why any five (5) amendments were considered necessary.

Materials: Several American history or government textbooks written on different reading levels, teacher-prepared print materials on different reading levels, films, filmstrips, tapes, teacher-made worksheets, crossword puzzles, and teacher-made games (How a Bill Becomes a Law, Checks and Balances game, Concentration games, Sentence Cards).

Introductory
Comment: This unit was developed to use with "school-level," or non-college preparatory track, junior high students whose reading levels range from third grade to seventh grade. Since the majority of school-level students in the past have had difficulty with the content of this unit, the teachers felt that utilizing the individualized learning-contract method would be the most effective way to deal with this subject. Each of the two classes which piloted these materials contained a mainstreamed child who had been earlier diagnosed as emotionally disturbed-learning disabled. Each spent some part of each day in a resource room with a Special Education teacher.

The individualized learning-contract method motivated all of the students because the learning process became enjoyable, and the pressure of learning what everyone else was learning at the same time and same pace was removed. There was a deadline for the entire packet of materials, but the work was done at each student's own tempo. The two mainstreamed students had no difficulty with either process or content; and, in fact, their behavior was exemplary, unlike what it had often been in class.

The sample contract and required assignments list which follow provided the structure for the open classroom model for mainstreaming. The students were required to complete correctly the various worksheets; and the information was available from books and other readings, tapes, films and filmstrips, games, and puzzles. Upon finishing each worksheet, the student presented it to the teacher for credit. Credit was not granted until the work-sheet was totally correct; students could consult sources again to rectify their errors.

Part I: Constitution

Required Assignments for Unit on the U.S. Constitution: Required of All Students

I. You must do all of the following worksheets:

1. "Word Association"
   — Day 1—Full class
2. "Predictive Statements on Law and Government"
   — Day 2—Full class
3. "The Making of a New Government"
4. "Representative Democracy"
5. "Compromises"
6. "Compromises"
7. "Branches of Government"
8. "Branches of Government"
9. "Federalism"
10. "Ratifying the Constitution"
    — Chart
11. "Bill of Rights"

II. Vocabulary Words—Define each and then use each in a sentence that you create.

III. Filmstrip—You must view the filmstrip on the "Bill of Rights."

Part II: Constitutional Contracts

The following is a contract between you and your Social Studies teacher. You are agreeing to fulfill all of Part I, the first page, and follow the directions on this page to receive a grade of 90% (ninety percent).* Your grade may go up or down 5 points, according to your own work.

1. *Games* — You must play *EACH* of the following games until you *WIN* at each game at least three (3) times.
   a. "Amendments"
   b. "Articles of Confederation"
   c. "Structure of the Constitution"
   d. "How a Bill Becomes a Law"
   e. "Sentences"
   f. "Checks and Balances"
2. *Filmstrips* — You must watch both of these filmstrips.
   a. "Part I—Origins of the Constitution"
   b. "Part II—Origins of the Constitution"
3. *Tape* — You must listen to the following tape.
   a. "Deciding Whether to Adopt the Constitution"
4. *Extra Worksheets* — Do two (2) of the following three (3) worksheets.
   a. #12—"How a Law Affects Our Lives" b. #13—"Crossword Puzzle"
   c. #14—"Chart of Adopting the Constitution"
5. *Cartoons* — Draw a cartoon on one (1) of the two (2) topics below.
   a. Compromises   b. Shays' Rebellion
6. *Extra Credit* — if you have finished everything else and you wish to do some extra work before the time limit is up, see your teacher.

I AGREE TO DO ALL THAT IS REQUIRED IN THIS CONTRACT.

SIGNED _____
(student's name)

Class _____ 3

*Other contracts are available to the student to earn 70% or 80%.
**Editor's note: Worksheets, crossword puzzle, etc. were not included due to space limitations.

Mainstreaming at Yorktown Heights High School

Thomas F. Howard and Alan Waidelich

We consider the three major concerns of mainstreaming to be the student, the classroom teacher, and the resource teacher; and we utilize the curriculum as a focal point for high school social studies. This appears to be oversimplified; however, if the purpose of mainstreaming is to provide the handicapped pupil with the same learning atmosphere as other students, then what is taught and how it is taught become vital points.

Of equal importance are the teachers themselves. Classroom teachers have depth in their subject areas, and this is their primary day-by-day teaching. On the other hand, Special Education teachers (Resource Room Teachers) work with students in, perhaps, four or five subject areas per day and probably do not have depth in more than one content area. They must rely heavily on lessons and materials from the classroom teachers. This does limit how much "beyond" the lesson they can go with their students.

We have found an Awareness Approach to be most helpful. Rather than water down a history curriculum, or abandon history altogether, we use this approach for all students, including the mainstreamed. *The learning atmosphere is identical for all.*

We start with the student's society today, with units covering a wide variety of topics affecting society, such as social problems involving controls, conflicts, change, corruption, rights of woman, city deterioration, and many others. *Each unit deals with some area of real concern to the student.* He or she is, after all, a citizen of our society. *We then work with parallels in past societies.*

Consider the problem from this viewpoint: What approach will give the student a view of history that will have meaning in his or her life today? To what can the student relate? What understandings are essential to the student?

The Awareness Approach is not a limited study of sociology; it is more than that. If we consider the history of Europe as a study of *past societies,* then why not examine *many* aspects of those societies? Certainly, people living in groups with governments, scientific discoveries, cultural achievements, economic systems, wars, and continual changes have impact upon other groups. History is an important aspect of society; herein lies its real value to the student. The same is true of art, literature, music, political science, and economics.

The following are features of this approach:

1. It is readily adaptable to the Individualized Educational Plan, without sacrificing the curriculum for all students — no cutting corners and no watering down.
2. In dealing with society today, the Resource Teacher does not have to have knowledge in depth of history or sociology. The situations are those we are aware of and which we recognize.
3. The information is available in school and local libraries, newspapers, magazines, and television.
4. Each of the units fits well into skills development.
5. The parents of the student can give valuable aid. History might not be their area of expertise. However, they can read newspapers and magazines with the student, as well as watch television together, and talk about what they read, see, and hear.
6. The examination of the past societies is structured enough for the mainstreamed student to follow in class (he or she does have focal points from today); and, just as important, he or she can make a contribution in discussions and questions.
7. In examining both present and past, in parallel, more activities become available, especially in small-group work. The student can be a contributing member of a team, and *that* is learning atmosphere.[4]

Integration and Learning Options

Linda Biemer

I do not believe that one separate lesson should be prepared to accommodate the mainstreamed student, who will then sit at one side of the classroom and do her or his work while all the other students complete a common lesson with the teacher. Nor should the teacher make no exceptions for the mainstreamed child, who, at first, probably will not satisfactorily complete the regular class lesson. Rather, the approach [I] advocate argues for both fully integrating the mainstreamed child into the regular class and class curriculum, and at the same time making available varied learning options for *all* students—the mainstreamed as well as the "more normal," the slow learner, and even the gifted child, all of whom are usually together in the regular class. The open classroom model would facilitate such an approach. The general classroom environment, therefore, includes learning or materials centers—one for textbooks, a second for filmstrips, a third for audiotapes, a fourth for primary source materials, a fifth for artifacts, and others. Students work individually or with one or more other students, and at their own pace.

While the students work independently of the teacher, the teacher's main role becomes that of facilitator, aiding mainstreamed and other students on a one-to-one basis, if necessary. Thus, all students are afforded the opportunity for individual help from the teacher. The use of this open classroom approach, therefore, assuages one of the major criticisms and fears parents of non-handicapped children have—namely, that the regular teacher will slight their child in order to spend more time with each child who has a disability.

The greatest amount of teacher time and effort actually goes into the preparation of each unit: (1) finding available print materials: texts, novels, biographies, primary source readings, newspapers, magazines, etc.; (2) making, locating, or ordering in advance appropriate audio, visual, and audio-visual materials and games; and (3) developing the learning activities themselves. The same objectives are to be met by all students, yet different activities are to be available which match the needs, abilities, learning styles, and interests of all students. Whether the teacher assigns students particular activities or whether the students select them themselves is an instructional decision to be made by the teacher, perhaps after experimenting with each approach.[5]

"Each One All Together" Project, Franklin, Tennessee

Tee Billingsley

A program has been developed to coordinate classroom activities with the services a child receives in special classes, such as Title I and Special Education classes. An intensive perceptual development program is used with kindergarten students to prepare them for a formal reading program in first grade. A K-1 transitional has been formed to provide additional readiness activities for students needing extra time before beginning a first-grade curriculum. All students not attending kindergarten will be placed in this class.[6]

Specifically, two units at the kindergarten level (How Do People Travel? and Where Am I?) stress skill development and experiences that prepare for a formal reading program. The strong feature is the integration and cooperation of a number of support services to assist each child in the initial experience in school.

Synergistic Classroom Model

Charles Meisgeier[7]

This is a comprehensive delivery plan which calls for educational planning to meet the unique needs of the learning disabled adolescent. [Professor Meisgeier has fully developed programs that can be used to implement mainstreaming in secondary schools. Rather than report on the four program components (which can be obtained by contacting Professor Meisgeier), a brief summary is offered.] The program suggests multisensory presentations; summarized, expanded, or highlighted presentations; and non-reading substitutions. The procedures fall into two categories. The first, methods to be adopted, includes: lecture, reading assignments, discussion, audiovisual presentation, and experiments/ student demonstration. The second relates to potential adaptations/ alternatives and deals with such activities and advanced organizers as: audio tapes, pertinent questions, highlighting, and shared note-taking. The program also stresses suitable evaluation techniques, appropriate behavior management procedures, environmental accommodations, and the mentor system. The comprehensive program has two components that will be of interest to social studies educators: social-behavioral and content mastery programs.

Five Generalizations

1. The comment that is consistently repeated, and usually the first suggestion offered, is the need for preplanning. Schools and teachers must prepare—and, to some degree, retool—to cope successfully with this new educational development. School districts must: develop and delineate roles; make inventories of available support services; identify services not offered but needed; conduct inservice education programs; establish groups of professionals; begin the process of developing a team approach; inventory educational materials and equipment; acquire needed materials and equipment; and conduct a community survey to find individuals and/or groups to support mainstreaming. Teachers also emphasize the necessity of adequate preplanning of social studies lessons and units. Classroom practitioners indicate that time and effort expended in organizing content and materials and in communicating these to ancillary personnel are critical elements in mainstreaming.

2. Teachers and ancillary-support people deliver another important message: "Individualization of instruction is the key to success in mainstreaming." The emphasis on the least restrictive environment requires that each child, whether handicapped or not, has the opportunity for success and growth. Personalized prescriptions are inherent in both the Individual Education Plan and the Individual Education Program. Individualization can be achieved by devoting time, attention, and resources to all of the elements listed in the preceding preplanning discussion. In brief, a range of options, materials, equipment, and personnel, both within and without the school, are necessary for individualization of instruction in the least restrictive environment.

3. Teachers state the need to have multisensory experiences and varied activities as the basis of social studies classroom instruction. The notion of multiple paths to learning—that each child learns in, by, and through different input processes—is the basis for appropriate procedures for each child. The success that is engendered becomes the motivator for further exploration and interaction to remove, or at least alleviate, student learning deficient areas. The interrelationship of this concept to preplanning and individualization reinforces the need to generate a wider classroom learning environment.

4. Some classroom teachers feel that the introduction of handicapped youngsters in the classroom will be a burden. This feeling is exacerbated if that youngster presents problems or conditions that engender feelings of inadequacy in teachers. Teachers who have experienced success in mainstreaming stress the need for support systems and people to assist in the development of appropriate learning environments, materials, and instructional procedures. As indicated in Chapter 1, a team approach to assist the teacher is a key ingredient for success. The team provides the teacher with data on the child's problem,

suggestions on appropriate instructional procedures and materials, and assistance in securing support equipment, materials, and services. Teachers thus become part of a larger team and do not deal with the problems of handicapped children in isolation. Teachers felt the urgent need for these arrangements, but they also expressed feelings of discomfort and insecurity in operating in a new team setting.

5. A fifth major point noted by teachers relates to parent and community involvement. The school and teacher cannot furnish all of the services, reinforcement, and practices needed by handicapped children to overcome their deficiencies. Although the sign-off of IEPs creates some concern on the part of teachers, this arrangement does provide a means for parent involvement in and support for the educational plan and program individually designed for the child. The handicapped child has a mechanism that enables all — teacher, school, home, and community — to deal with and overcome the condition. While teachers point out that more meetings and paper work are included in the day, they also state that the concentration of support services is a significant asset to the teaching-learning situation.

Mainstreaming creates a new set of conditions — organizationally and instructionally — for teachers. They express feelings of anxiety and inadequacy, but they also communicate exhilaration at measures of success with handicapped children in mainstreamed classes.

Footnotes

[1] Entire section is from a paper submitted by Thomas F. Banit of Walpole High School, Walpole, Massachusetts and Eileen J. Cunningham of the Sudbury Public Schools, Sudbury, Massachusetts.

[2] This entire plan was submitted by Michele M. Paoletti of Woodhaven Schools, Inc., of Columbia, Missouri.

[3] This plan was submitted by Linda Biemer of SUNY Binghamton, New York, and Gail Abraham and Ronald Pierce of African Road Junior High School, Vestal, New York.

[4] Entire section is from a paper submitted by Thomas Howard and Alan Waidelich.

[5] Entire section is from a paper submitted by Linda Biemer.

[6] Quote is from materials submitted by Tee Billingsley of the Williamson County Schools, Franklin, Tennessee.

[7] For further information on the "Synergistic Classroom Model," contact Professor Charles Meisgeier, University of Houston, Houston, Texas 77004.

"Discuss means and ways to make public facilities more accessible to handicapped individuals."

8.Involving the Community

Ramon M. Rocha and Robert L. Marion

The major premise of the mainstreaming movement is that the handicapped can be reintegrated into the mainstream of community living. For the most part, the community readily accepts mainstreaming for those individuals who are mildly handicapped and who appear to the public not to deviate significantly from the general population either in actions or physical appearance.

The problem of community integration is more difficult for those who are moderately to severely handicapped. The individual who has spent years living in an institutional setting generally has handicapping conditions that tend to make the person more dependent on others. There are notable exceptions, however; those who suffered from epilepsy were often institutionalized because the public found them "threatening and dangerous."

The moral dilemma of reintegrating the handicapped into the commuity is that some people who advocate more humane treatment and conditions for those faceless individuals in institutions often violently oppose practicing what they rhetorically support. The objections to integrating the handicapped, particularly the moderately retarded, have led to law suits and other actions.

In the lessons presented, the teacher should use the community to teach about problems associated with mainstreaming the handicapped into the communtiy. This series of lessons involves activities that will require students to examine their own attitudes and prejudices towards the handicapped and to become more involved with the communtiy. As a result of these activities (films, speakers, etc.), it is hoped that the students will recognize that the handicapped do not differ significantly from the "normal" population. Also, these lessons may teach the youth of today to accept the handicapped in their rightful place—their community.

Community Involvement

Community involvement is a value-laden term. This is most evident in the field of education, where divergent viewpoints have been voiced by the community. When children with special needs are served, it seems to evoke positive and negative reactions from the community. Nowhere else in education has the community viewpoint been recognized more than in Special Education, the area of education that serves the handicapped or exceptional child. (See the newspaper clippings — Figure 1, p. 68.) However, regardless of the attitude held by people, the decade of the 1970s has focused attention upon the handicapped. Therefore, if the community holds a positive perspective of the handicapped, it is to the educator's advantage; and community involvement is easier to achieve. If the handicapped/exceptional child is viewed in a negative light, educators are obligated to take action to correct any erroneous impressions existing in the community. Social studies educators are in a unique position to facilitate changes in negative attitudes or to reinforce positive opinions concerning the handicapped.

The field of social studies has the capacity to work with children, parents, and the community to foster a greater understanding of P.L. 94-142 (Education of the Handicapped Act of 1975) and to promote a greater acceptance of the concept of mainstreaming or least restrictive environments. Social studies teachers are assured of a measure of success if they: (1) use the resources of the community to teach about the community, (2) create an awareness in the community about the needs of the handicapped, (3) make learning skills relevant to the students by using the community as a social studies laboratory, and (4) maximize available school and community resources and materials into a comprehensive program.

Elementary and secondary teachers can utilize the previous guidelines to derive teacher/learner goals and objectives. More specifically, social studies teachers might have the following teacher/learner goals in mind when addressing the problem of community involvement. Goals could be identified as:

(1) to find and use information sources about the community
(2) to identify specific resources, their locations, and the services they provide

(3) to identify feelings regarding use of these services by the handicapped

(4) to become aware of the types of jobs and their availability to the handicapped

(5) to demonstrate the formal and informal political and social climate of the community and its effect on the handicapped.

Using the above goals, the teacher can facilitate learner skills in the areas of communication and problem solving. In the area of communication, the skills of interviewing, functional reading, telephone usage, and writing can be developed. Problem-solving skills in the area of map usage, consumer finance, and legal aid can also become practical outcomes.

Following this approach, the social studies teacher (elementary and secondary) can combine the cognitive and affective bases of instruction utilizing the community. The lesson plans presented on the following pages are intended to serve as illustrations for a two-week unit.

Using the Community To Teach About the Community
Exploring the Attitudes of the Community Toward the Handicapped

Day 1 What are the attitudes towards the handicapped in your community?

Elementary Activity

You (teacher) read or have students read a series of headlines from the area, town, or city newspaper related to the handicapped in the community. Discuss with students the sentiments expressed in the headlines. Examples: "Mentally Retarded Can Be Good Neighbors."

Assignment: Assign each student an article (provided by you) that relates to the treatment of the handicapped for discussion with his or her parents or parent.

Study Questions:

(1) How are handicapped people treated in your community?
(2) Are most "normal people" afraid of handicapped people?

Secondary Activity

You (teacher) should present a series of headlines taken from your area newspaper related to the handicapped in your community. Have the students discuss the sentiment expressed in the headlines. For example: "Mentally Retarded Can Be Good Neighbors."

Assignment: Assign each student to read one newspaper article (provided by you) related to the treatment of the handicapped in the community.

Study Questions:

(1) How are the handicapped people in your community treated?
(2) Why do "normal" people feel "threatened" by handicapped people?

Day 2 Elementary Activity

Begin class activities with a discussion about their families' reactions to the articles. Follow-up with additional discussions and answers about the study questions.

Assignment: Have students discuss their own feelings about the handicapped. Relate their feelings to sentiments expressed or not expressed in the articles.

Secondary Activity

Begin discussion with students about their readings. Follow this with answering and discussing the two study questions.

Assignment: Have each student individually answer the worksheet provided. After this has been done, group the students into clusters of three or four and have them discuss their solutions. *Note:* Each of the group members will need a copy of the same article. Your should, however, have articles covering four or more topics. (See Student Handout—Figure 2.)

Figure 2. Student Handout

Name _____

Directions: Read through the article provided to you and complete the worksheet. As a group, you will also have to identify and agree on the problem and the most viable solution.

1. Define the major problem outlined in the article. _____

_____

2. List alternative solutions to the problem. In arriving at your solution, you must consider cost factors, time involved, human resources needed, community attitudes, etc.

A. _____

B. _____

C. _____

D. _____

3. If you used solution A, what would you expect to happen? _____

_____

If you used solution B, what would you expect to happen? _____

_____

If you used solution C, what would you expect to happen? _____

_____

If you used solution D, what would you expect to happen? _____

_____

4. Choose the solution which best solves the problem. Explain why you and your group selected this solution rather than the others. Be prepared to defend your solution.

Day 3 Elementary Activity

Review previous days' discussions about the handicapped. Assist students to identify what the local community is doing to accommodate the needs of the handicapped. Discuss the reasons that some things are being done as a result of legislation and others are being done to comply with legal decisions of the court.

Assignment: Have each student interview a neighbor on the two questions asked in lesson #1.

Children should ask parents to accompany them. In this manner, parents can make sure that neighbors are aware that it is a school social studies assignment, and that children are not representing any agency or soliciting support for a community facility for the handicapped.

Secondary Activity

Begin the period by having each group identify what it perceived to be the major problem. Also have the group relate their solutions to the problem (s).

At this time you should introduce ways to identify what your local community is doing to accommodate the needs of the handicapped. It should be pointed out that some of the things that are being done are a result of legislation.

Activity: Assign each student to use the survey instrument to gain information in his or her own home neighborhood. Each student should be required to interview five adults, preferably homeowners. In conducting the interviews, the students should explain that this survey is part of a social studies assignment to learn more about community attitudes towards the handicapped. It should be stressed that the students do not represent any agency and that there is no proposal to establish a residence for handicapped individuals in the neighborhood.

Survey Questionnaire

1. Is it your opinion that handicapped individuals would be better served in the community than in institutions?
2. Do you know how much it costs to maintain an individual in a state institution per year? Would you care to estimate the cost?*
3. In your opinion, is our community able and willing to meet adequately the needs of people who were once institutionalized and are now returning to the community?
4. Would you approve and support the establishment of a community residence for the mentally retarded in your neighborhood? If not, why not?

*Approximate cost is $12,000 per year per resident.

Day 4 Elementary and Secondary Activity: (Same)

Invite a speaker(s) from one or more of the following agencies to discuss the handicapping conditions of their clients and how their needs are being met by the community and, in particular, by the agencies that the speakers represent.
Community agencies found in most areas include:
> Association for Retarded Citizens
> Association for the Blind
> Office of Vocational Rehabilitation
> United Cerebral Palsy Association
> Association for Children with Learning Disabilities

Day 5 Elementary Activity

Discuss with the students the results of their interviews with neighbors. Have the students summarize differences and similarities between parents' and neighbors' viewpoints. Discuss why these differences and similarities might exist in the same community. Relate these to the comments of the speakers of the previous day.

Secondary Activity

Each student should tabulate and analyze his or her results. A group could then generate a report on the entire class' results. Discuss the results of the survey questionnaire. Have students summarize the results of their findings. Ask them to explain not only what they recorded in terms of response, but also to describe "feelings and attitudes" they perceived.

Day 6 Elementary and Secondary Activities: (Same)

Provide a simulation activity to experience what it might be like to be handicapped. For this lesson you may wish to enlist the help of some of the speakers and the agencies they represent.
Materials would include:
> A. wheelchairs
> B. blindfolds
> C. canes
> D. sign language cards (Bliss Symbolics)

Activities could include:
> A. Having students get from the curb/sidewalk outside the school to the class in the wheelchair or wearing blindfold.
> B. Manipulating a wheelchair into toilet and toilet stall.
> C. Using public telephone from a wheelchair.
> D. Using sign language cards to express needs without using expressive language.
> E. Having students dress themselves (socks, shoes, shirt) with one arm strapped to their body.

Day 7—8 Elementary and Secondary Activity: (Same)

Have students complete a Checklist of Accessibility in the school and in at least one public building; i.e., post office in the community.

Activity; For this activity it might be best to form dyads. Each pair will need a tape measure. Use the Checklist of Accessibility — Figure 3 to record information.

Figure 3. Checklist of Accessibility

Name of Site _____   Name of Inspector _____

Address of Site _____   Date of Inspection _____

_____

Instructions: Mark a __✓__ for YES, mark an __x__ for NO,
leave blank ____ for DOES NOT APPLY

WALKS:
Sidewalks are 48 inches wide, min. ___
Maximum slope of walks is 1-in-20 ___
Walks are not interrupted by steps ___
Level area at doorways is 5' x 5' min. ___

PARKING:
Special spaces near entrance ___
Sign saying reserved for handicapped ___
Sign also has wheelchair symbol ___
Level area suitable for wheelchairs ___
Special spaces are 12 feet wide ___
Adequate number of special spaces ___

RAMPS:
Slope at 1-in-12, maximum ___
Ramps have railings on both sides ___
Railings are 33" high ___
Railings extend 1 foot beyond ends ___
Railing cross-section is round or oval ___
Railing section 1¼" diam., min., 2" max. ___
Railing clearance is 1½" from wall ___
Ramp surface is non-slippery when wet ___
Level area at doors is 6' x 5', min. ___
Ramps extend 5 ft. at bottom ___
Level platform in ramp every 34 ft., max. ___
Level platform in ramp at all turns ___

ENTRANCES:
At least 1 entrance OK by wheelchair ___
At least 1 entrance OK to elevators ___
Entrance vestibule 7 ft. deep, min. ___

Entrance vestibule at least 1 ft. wider than single-door width ___

DOORS:
Each door 3 feet wide minimum ___
Doors open with 15 pound force, max. ___
Exterior thresholds ½" high, max. ___
No interior thresholds ___
Level area at door 5' x 5' min., ea. side ___

IDENTIFICATION BY BLIND:
Raised or recessed letters at exits, stairs, toilets, elevators, room names ___
Locate signs 5'-0" to 5'-6" high ___
Locate signs on or near doors ___
Knurled hardware at doors to danger: loading docks, boiler room, stages, electric rooms, etc. ___
Fire alarms have visual & audio signal ___

PLACES OF ASSEMBLY:
2% seating reserved for wheelchairs ___
Cafeteria, vending usable by wheelchair ___

IDENTIFICATION:
Use Wheelchair Symbol if accessible ___
Symbol at accessible entrance ___
Symbol pointing to accessible entrance ___
Symbol at accessible toilets ___
Symbol and sign at special parking spaces ___

(Continued on p. 74)

STAIRS:
No projection of tread beyond riser ___
Riser may slope 1¼ inch, max. ___
Stairs 3'-6" wide, min. ___
No wedge-shaped steps ___
Railings on both sides of stairs ___
Railings 33" high ___
Railings extend 18" beyond top and
  bottom step ___
Railing ends are at height of 36" ___
Railing cross-section is round or oval ___
Railing section 1¼" diam., min., 2"
  max. ___
Railing clearance is 1½" from wall ___

FLOOR:
Floor surface is non-slippery when
  wet ___
Floor is of one common level, or
  ramped ___

TOILETS:
Toilets are on ea. floor for ea. sex ___
Space for wheelchair to turn around ___
Vestibule doors are 3 ft. wide ___
Vestibule 4' wide x 6' long, min. ___
Each toilet has 1 stall for wheelchair
  use ___
a) Stall size is 5'-6" x 6' ___
b) Stall door is 3' wide, swinging out ___
c) Stall has 2 grab bars 4' long 3'
   high, 1 at rear, 1 at side nearest
   toilet ___
d) Toilet seat is 18 inches high ___
e) Toilet is centered 18" from near
   wall ___
Sink has no legs or pedestal ___

Sink has 30" clearance under rim ___
Bottom of mirror over sink is 40"
  high, max. ___
Shelf over sink is 40" high, max. ___
Urinal rim no higher than 15" ___
All wall dispensers are usable at 40"
  max. ___

WATER FOUNTAINS:
Water spout is at the front ___
Push-button control, not spring-
  action ___
If wall-mounted, 34" to rim, max. ___
If floor-mounted and rim is higher
  than 34", provide paper cups or
  another lower fountain ___

PUBLIC TELEPHONES:
Coin slots 54" high, maximum ___
Enclosure permits use from wheel-
  chair ___

ELEVATORS:
Does building have elevator? ___
How many public floor levels has
  bldg? ___
Door opening is 32" wide, minimum ___
Cab size is 4' x 4'-6", minimum ___
Controls are 60" high, maximum ___
Controls have raised or recessed
  numbers ___

CONTROLS:
Switches & controls 40" min., 48"
  max. ___
Thermostats, intercoms, fire alarms
  56" max. ___

(Architectual Accessibility for the Disabled of College Campuses. State University
Construction Fund. Albany, N.Y., 1967.)

Day 9 Elementary and Secondary Activity: (Same)

Students report the results of the findings gathered in assessing accessibility. (Use similar procedures as in Day 5.) Discuss means and ways to make public facilities more accessible to handicapped individuals. It would be beneficial to develop this list into recommendations that could be presented to the school administration and school board.

Day 10 Elementary and Secondary Activity: (Same)

Select one of the three films listed [at the end of this chapter] and view it. Each of the films suggests problems related to community barriers and attitudinal barriers that limit the growth and development of the handicapped. Small group and/or whole class discussion should follow on a key question(s) provided before viewing the film.

Conclusion

Involving the community as a resource for teaching about the handicapped can easily become an integral part of the teacher/learner process in social studies education. The living laboratory of the community has the potential to allow social studies teachers the opportunity to promote acceptance of differences among individuals. By involving the community, the social studies teacher also has the ability to provide enjoyable and adaptable learning experiences for students and adults concerning the handicapped/exceptional person. After exposure to this community awareness unit, the learners and their parents will become more intelligent consumers of information concerning the handicapped.

Films

Coming Home deals with the controversial issue of deinstitutionalization and the establishment of community residences for the retarded. This film is an accurate portrayal of prejudices and fears associated with the retarded living in the community. Available from: Motion Picture Enterprises, Tarrytown, N.Y. 10952. For secondary or adult audiences.

Graduation is a documentary film that describes the lack of community post-school services for the moderately retarded. Available from: Motion Picture Enterprises, Tarrytown, N.Y. 10952.

Try Another Way, narrated by Dr. Marc Gold, emphasizes that the vocational potential of the retarded is underestimated. He stresses the need for more accurate assessment and instruction. Available from: Motion Picture Enterprises, Tarrytown, N.Y. 10952.

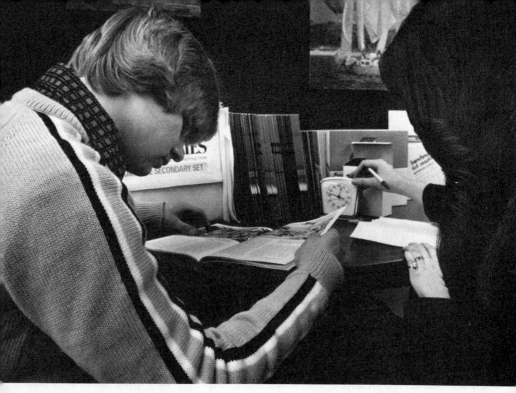

Resource room teacher assisting mainstreamed secondary student with social studies lesson.

9. Effective Inservice Education

Thomas M. Skrtic, Frances L. Clark, and H. Earle Knowlton

The National Advisory Committee on the Handicapped estimated that 260,000 Special Education personnel and over two million regular educators require inservice training to implement P.L. 94-142.[1] The Bureau of Education for the Handicapped identified inservice training as a national priority and allocated over 48 percent (or $26,858,000) of its 1979 Personnel Preparation budget for inservice education.[2] The importance of inservice training to the implementation of P.L. 94-142 was recognized by the authors of the law when they made compliance contingent upon the ability of each state to develop and implement a comprehensive system of personnel development.[3]

Guidelines for Effective Inservice Education[4]

Over the past 130 years, inservice education has been approached from both *remedial* and *continuous growth* points of view.[5] Despite the development of the concept of teacher education as continuous professional development over 100 years ago, its application to inservice education has yet to be realized.[6] While numerous condemnations of inservice education exist in the literature, few authors have provided direction for positive change. The delivery of inservice education which will prepare educators to teach handicapped students in regular class-rooms must represent a drastic departure from past inservice efforts. Six guidelines for the development of effective inservice education are presented in the following paragraphs.[7]

1. *Inservice education related to the education of handicapped students should be based on an assessment of the strengths and needs of local regular and Special Education personnel.* The involvement of social studies and Special Education personnel in determining the content of inservice education programs should be sought not only as the programs are initially designed, but also during implementation to ensure a responsiveness to their changing needs.

2. *Regular and Special Education personnel should assume roles as planners and teachers of inservice programs.* While the traditional design of inservice activities places school personnel in the role of learners, they could and should assume leadership roles in the planning and delivery of inservice education. Many social studies educators and Special Educators can effectively design and deliver inservice education for their peers.

3. *Inservice education programs should provide participants with many different ways to accomplish their individual goals.* Within inservice education programs for social studies educators, opportunities should exist for individuals to select from a number of alternative activities those which meet their needs. The concept of individually-tailored educational plans for handicapped students can be extended to the design of individual inservice plans for regular and Special Education personnel.

4. *Evaluation, an integral part of any educational endeavor, should examine the impact of inservice education on participants' behavior and, ultimately, on student performance.* Evaluation strategies should be designed to examine participants' attitudes, knowledge, skills, and behaviors; resulting impact on student performance; and parental satisfaction with the student's program.

5. *Local education agencies must make a commitment to the concept of continuing professional development through implementation of an on-going, coordinated inservice program.* A program which presents content in a coordinated, ongoing effort, rather than in "single-shot" sessions, will demonstrate a district's commitment to move beyond compliance with P.L. 94-142 to meet the *intent* of the law.

6. *Inservice education should be a collaborative effort which recognizes and uses the strengths of LEAs, SEAs, IHEs, and POs.* Cooperative involvement of all agencies, as well as a realistic appraisal of the strengths each agency brings to the situation, will facilitate the design and delivery of an inservice program which capitalizes on these strengths.

The following section will present a model for inservice education which is based on these guidelines. This approach to inservice education emphasizes the philosophy that local educational personnel can and should respond to their own training needs.

A Model for Inservice Education

While P.L. 94-142 has generated substantial content, a structure for the development and delivery of this content which is consistent with the guidelines for effective inservice education is needed. Recently, a model has been proposed to facilitate the provision of effective inservice education.[8] This model, based on the curriculum development process, can be used by regular and Special Education personnel to design and deliver inservice education related to the education of handicapped students. The process of curriculum development involves the: (a) identification of needs, (b) specification and validation of objectives, (c) design of learning activities, (d) delivery of instruction, and (e) evaluation of that instruction.

The inservice education model as outlined here can be implemented on a state-wide, regional, or individual district level. Through the collaborative efforts of the SEAs, IHEs, POs, and LEAs, inservice education can be developed for several districts within a state, for several districts within an intermediate education agency, or for several schools within a district.

The procedures for implementation of the curriculum development approach to inservice education are described as they relate to three major phases of activities: Planning, Curriculum Development Training, and Content Delivery (see Figure 1).

Planning Activities

During the planning phase, the foundation for cooperation among agencies is established, and the nature of each agency's involvement is delineated. An appraisal of the contributions each group can make to the total inservice effort will allow the recognition and use of the strengths of each agency. Several important tasks must be completed at this time, including: (a) the identification of the target population (teachers, administrators, school psychologists, etc.), (b) the identification of competencies (from published lists and/or knowledge of specific district needs), (c) the selection of teams of teachers to serve as inservice planners and trainers, and (d) the identification and review of existing inservice packages. Also during this phase, a curriculum development training program designed to train educators to serve as inservice planners and trainers must be identified and/or developed by the cooperating agency or agencies skilled in curriculum development. Through this training, educators will acquire the skills necessary to fulfill the roles of inservice planner and trainer as they design inservice programs for their colleagues.

Curriculum Development Training

During this aspect of the inservice education program, curriculum development team members are trained to design, develop, and deliver inservice education for their peers.

Figure 1. Inservice Education Model
A Curriculum Development Approach

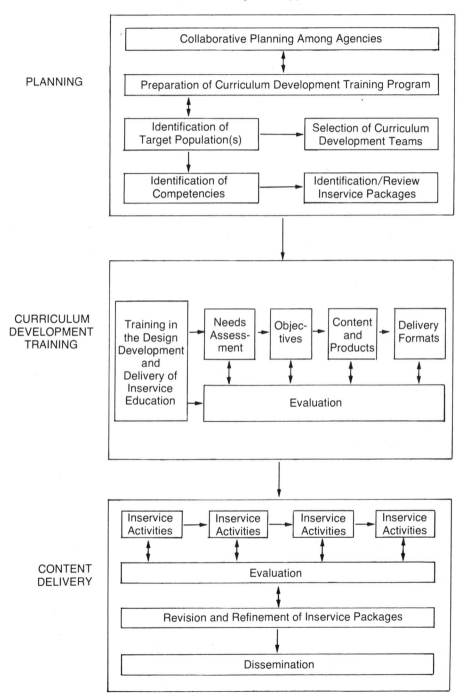

Initially, team members are trained in (a) the design, administration, and interpretation of needs assessment instrumentation, and (b) the specification of local needs. Team members will then implement these procedures and analyze results. Following the specification of needs, team members are trained to write objectives based on identified local needs and to validate these objectives with their peers.

During the final phase of curriculum development training, team members are trained to (a) adopt, adapt, and/or develop appropriate content and delivery formats for inservice activities, (b) deliver the inservice content, and (c) select, modify, and/or design procedures to evaluate inservice programs.

The advantage of the curriculum development approach is that it facilitates the development of activities based on the needs of teachers related to implementing their local social studies curriculum with handicapped students. In most instances, social studies educators will not require inservice education in social studies curriculum itself, but in the delivery of that curriculum to handicapped students; i.e., instructional procedures for handicapped students. However, Special Educators who work cooperatively with social studies educators will benefit from inservice education in the social studies curriculum. The team approach to the development of the inservice activities allows the merger of the social studies curriculum (brought by the social studies educator) and instructional techniques for handicapped students (brought by the Special Educator). Collaboration between these two individuals will lead not only to the refinement of the instructional techniques for implementation in the social studies classroom, but also to the development of inservice activities to train their peers in the implementation of the techniques.

Content Delivery

The most extensive activity in the implementation of the inservice program is the delivery of content designed to address the needs of social studies and Special Education personnel. Curriculum development team members coordinate the content, delivery, and evaluation of inservice sessions. Both team members and representatives of designated agencies are involved in evaluation and follow-up activities as social studies and Special Education personnel apply new knowledge and skills. A description of the evaluation component of this inservice model is found in Skrtic, Knowlton, and Clark.[9]

Traditionally, instructional personnel, including social studies teachers, have not assumed roles as planners and trainers in inservice education. They have been consumers of inservice education attempts which, in general, have been characterized as ineffective. P.L. 94-142 provides an opportunity for teachers to change the nature of staff development in the teaching profession. This chapter has attempted to describe a procedure for active, rather than passive, involvement in the staff development process.

Conclusions

While many inservice efforts will be offered and accepted as being in compliance with P.L. 94-142, the curriculum development approach enables the education profession to respond to the immediate *and* continuing challenge of staff development. Curriculum development skills acquired as a result of the implementation of this model can be generalized to many areas. The curriculum development process can be used to design inservice education related to specific subject areas; e.g., to train social studies teachers in techniques for inquiry learning, gaming, moral education, and the development of case studies. The skills may also be employed in the development or modification of curriculum; e.g., modification of regular education curriculum for handicapped students, the design of individual sequences of instruction for handicapped or non-handicapped students, and the design of curriculum in social studies or specific skills within that area (map and globe skills, decision-making skills, etc.).

Undoubtedly, the most significant contribution of the curriculum development approach is the development of a lasting resource at the LEA level.[10] While tangible products will result from the implementation of this approach, the intangible benefits to the professionalism and morale of staff members will have a much greater impact. The establishment of an atmosphere which encourages educators to grow and develop professionally, to be *captured* by an idea,[11] and to explore new avenues and approaches represents a valuable asset to schools and to the students they serve.

Footnotes

[1] Natonal Advisory Committee on the Handicapped, *The Individualized Education Program: Key to An Appropriate Education for the Handicapped Child, 1977 Annual Report* (Washington, D.C.: U.S. Government Printing Office, 1977).

[2] James Siantz and Edward Moore, "Inservice Programming and Preservice Priorities," in J. Smith, ed., *Personnel Preparation and Public Law 94-142: The Map, the Mission and the Mandate* (Boothwyn, Pennysylvania: Educational Resources Center, 1978).

[3] Section 613 (a) (3) (A). *Public Law 94-142, Education for All Handicapped Children Act,* November 29, 1975.

[4] A more complete discussion has been published in Thomas M. Skrtic, H. Earle Knowlton, and Frances L. Clark, "Action versus Reaction: A Curriculum Development Approach to Inservice Education," *Focus on Exceptional Children,* 1979, 11 (1).

[5] R. W. Tyler, "In-service Education of Teachers: A Look at the Past and Future," in L. J. Rubin, ed., *Improving In-service Education: Proposals and Procedures for Change* (Boston: Allyn and Bacon, 1971).

[6] See: R. A. Edelfelt and G. Lawrence, "In-service Education: The State of the Art," in R. A. Edelfelt and M. Johnson, eds., *Rethinking In-service Education* (Washington, D.C.: National Education Association, 1975), and L. J. Rubin, *Improving In-service Education: Proposals and Procedures for Change* (Boston: Allyn and Bacon, 1971).

[7] These guidelines represent a compilation of the following three sources: R. A. Edelfelt, ed., *Inservice Education: Criteria for and Examples of Local Programs* (Bellingham, Wash.: Western Washington State College, 1977); G. Lawrence, D. Baker, P. Elzie, and B. Hansen, *Patterns of Effective In-service Education: A State of the Art Summary of Research on Materials and Procedures of Changing Teacher Behaviors in In-service Education* (Gainesville, Fla: Florida State Department of Education, 1974); and James Siantz and Edward Moore, *op.cit.*

[8] Thomas M. Skrtic, H. Earle Knowlton, and Frances L. Clark, *op.cit.*

[9] *Ibid.*

[10] Edward L. Meyen, *Demonstration of Dissemination Practices on Special Class Instruction for the Mentally Retarded: Utilizing Master Teachers as In-service Educators. Volume II: Report on the Evaluation of Project Activities* (Project No. OEG 3-7-02883-04999, U.S. Department of Health, Education, and Welfare, Office of Education, Bureau of Education for the Handicapped, 1969).

[11] G. McDaniels, Address to Handicapped Children Model Program, October 23, 1978 (Printed in *Centering In,* Winter, 1978-79).

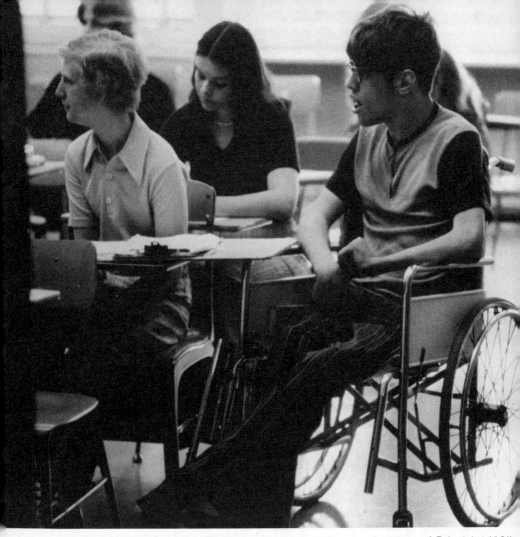

"What will be our record in 2000 A.D. on the silver anniversary of P.L. 94-142?"

10.Prologue for the Future

William T. Lowe

There is more conflict and dissension, even outright opposition, to the movement for mainstreaming than the authors of this Bulletin have noted. There are many opponents, including, as would be expected, some overwhelmed "regular" classroom teachers.[1] But, more surprising, attacks are also coming from leaders of and spokespersons for the handicapped, particularly the more severly disabled. For example, McCoy Vernon, the editor of *American Annals for the Deaf,* states in a heated editorial entitled "The Road to Hell,"[2] "Without doubt Public Law 94-142 is the most ill-conceived piece of legislation ever to pass through Congress." He goes on to insist that there are at least four major faults with the law: (1) there is inadequate funding, (2) there is promotion of "the naive assumption that mainstreaming is both feasible and desirable for the overwhelming majority of handicapped children," (3) it requires an overabundance of paper work and bureaucratic processing, and (4) it perpetuates a "cruel deception" that promises more than can possibly be delivered, (Even this militant critic, however, praises the intent of the law; it is the reality as he sees it that he attacks.) Some of the officials of the Council for Exceptional Children and the Bureau of Education for the Handicapped of HEW—two groups that were instrumental in developing P.L. 94-142—also have some serious doubts about the reality of implementing the law.[3] I also feel obliged to remind the reader that while we are moving toward mainstreaming the handicapped, there exists a widespread counter-movement to remove the gifted and talented from the mainstream—a curious contradiction. Notwithstanding these developments, social studies educators have an obligation to look ahead and to plan for the future.

The Future

Twenty-five years ago it was the Supreme Court, not the Congress, that presented a tremendous challenge concerning integration. During the years that followed, some modest progress was made, particularly in the South and the Southwest; but there is more racial isolation in most of our schools than before Brown. For an entire generation, there have been painful confrontations, even bloody ones, throughout the land; the Congress has recently passed anti-busing legislation; and about half of the members of the House of Representatives voted for a Constitutional Amendment that would have banned the use of buses to help desegregate our schools. No issue has been more divisive. We have largely failed to meet the test.

What will be our record in 2000 A.D. on the silver anniversary of P.L. 94-142?

Projection on such a question is complex and fraught with possibilities for error; prediction is downright foolhardy. Nevertheless, we ought to try, because of the significance of the issues. A number of authors from a variety of perspectives have made some projections, even predictions.[4] What follows is mainly a summary of two such studies coming from educational practitioners. There are also some editorial comments appearing in parentheses.

• Leaders of Special Education React

One hundred and twenty-one highly placed Special Education administrators representing the entire country reacted to two rounds of hypothetical occurrences by indicating the year in which they thought an event would occur and whether they thought this was a positive or negative development.[5] This study, using a modified Delphi technique, was sponsored by the National Association of State Directors of Special Education; and it was conducted in 1973-74 as the final work was being done on P.L. 94-142. Here are some of the results of the study paraphrased from the discussion section of the report. Viewing them as positive happenings likely during the next 25 years, the leaders predict that:

Plus

+ All exceptional children will be receiving formal educational services. (Only half were receiving such services at the time of the survey.)
+ Due process guarantees will be generally operative. Parents will be heavily involved. The courts will play a leadership role. (Some of the administrators find this threatening.)
+ A degree, at least, of uniformity of opportunities will exist across regional and state boundaries. (Certainly far from true now.)
+ States will administer sophisticated evaluations of special and general educational programs in both public and private schools. (Accountability in a formal sense will continue and expand.)
+ Laws guaranteeing employment parity for the handicapped will be passed and enforced. (Again, our litigiousness will be a major factor.)
+ More extensive child protection services will be mandated by law.
+ A greater variety of alternatives to the traditional school will be operating for all learners, but especially for handicapped ones.
+ Financing schools will be radically changed with the demise of the real estate property tax as a major base and with a more balanced sharing of costs by local, regional, state, and national sources. (Mainstreaming

will play a major role in this reformation—the courts again.)

+ Regionalism will continue to grow with sharing of resources and other elements among local districts. (This will be especially apparent in expensive services for the handicapped.)

+ Far more extensive use of technology to compensate for handicapping conditions will be made in the general classroom. Also, technological marvels will be developed to help the blind "see," the deaf "hear," and others to have comparable achievements.

+ Individualized/prescriptive instructional approaches will be in widespread use for all learners. (We certainly have heard this for years.)

+ The mainstreaming concept will be generally accepted by most citizens.(Perhaps, but . . .)

+ Preschool programs will be universally available. They will emphasize the identification of children with handicaps and will offer appropriate treatment and referrals. (Where is the money going to come from?)

+ The preservice preparation of all teachers will include at least six credits of work in Special Education. (What will be dropped?)

+ Continuing education will be a requirement for renewal of teacher certificates. (Certainly, the examination movement is booming.)

+ Year-round schools will be expanded, and this will greatly aid the handicapped since they often need more time to achieve. (A case is now being heard in Pennsylvania that would require local districts to offer full-year programs for those who need the extra time.)

The Special Education administrators also predict that the following events will occur, but they are displeased about these potential developments:

Minus

— The Supreme Court will rule compulsory school attendance as unconstitutional and this will have a negative impact on the availability of educational opportunities. (Think of it—fascinating.)

— The federal government will replace categorical funding with block grants. This action will ultimately reduce the funds available to handicapped learners. (This idea is repeated by citizen advocates, scholars, classroom teachers, and others—interesting.)

— Super-agencies will be created that are supposed to attend to the total needs—medical , psychological, educational, occupational, and others—of the handicapped.

(The educational administrators are clearly threatened by this thought.)
- There will be an increasing shortage of residential facilities for the severely handicapped. (Will schools for the deaf, for example, be forced to close? What will the impact be?)
- The federal government will take full financial responsibility for educating the handicapped. (A fear of big government comes through here.)
- A voucher system for the handicapped will be instituted. (A fear of too little government appears to be the motive here.)
- Non-habit forming drugs to accelerate learning will be widely used!
- Teachers unions will dominate the inservice training of teachers. Unions will have increasing power also in determining enrollments. (No mystery about why administrators fear this development.)

● **NEA Panel Reacts**

The National Education Association appointed a panel representing the Council for Exceptional Children, the National Association for the Deaf, the National Association of Secondary and Elementary School Principals, parents of handicapped children, and classroom teachers to examine the actual and potential impact of P.L. 94-142.[6] The study was published in 1978. After exploring areas of consensus, conflict, and challenge, the panel made numerous recommendations in a section entitled " Future Directions." (This report is highly recommended reading, and this writer believes that many of the NEA recommendations will become reality.) Here are some of the most significant:

● A systematic and vigorous effort should be made to identify and evaluate handicapped children in and out of school. Particular effort should be directed at economically disadvantaged youngsters.
● Greatly increased effort must be undertaken to reduce misclassification and detrimental labeling of persons. As a part of this effort, the use of group-administered, norm-referenced, standardized tests should be and will be discontinued. (Sounds like the 1960s.)
● Far greater emphasis should be placed on recruiting bilingual educators to serve at all levels in all capacities in school.
● Much expanded and improved teacher education must be instituted. State departments of education, teachers organizations, local and intermediate districts, colleges and universities, individual educators, and others have specified roles to play in this proposed development. All educators must have an opportunity to study and to work with exceptional learners.

• "Regular"teachers must be given more time to achieve the new roles required of them by mainstreaming. Conferring with others, preparing IEPs, processing the paper work, and doing other duties require hours that just are not available to already overworked teachers. Flexible scheduling could help and must be implemented.

• The NEA Panel does not wish to suggest a formula that might become rigid and oppressive, but it does recommend that class size be reduced when handicapped children are mainstreamed. (The Panel was fully aware of conflicting research on this subject, and it persuasively attacks it.)

• Appropriate supportive facilities must be readily available. Resource teachers, therapists, note-takers for the deaf, communications specialists, and many other personnel will need to be available. Also, equipment and facilities of a wide range must be accessible.

• The rights and responsibilities of teachers as well as those of learners must be specified and protected. Accountability is fine, but the classroom teacher must have the right to hold others accountable to him or her in the performance of his or her duties. (Not surprising, nor unreasonable.)

• Access to an appropriate education will involve massive changes in transportation facilities, building and grounds, instructional equipment, and other areas. Some districts are already making these modifications, and specific non-costly suggestions are offered.

• School-home communications must be greatly improved and teachers need time and additional skills to make these changes. (P.L. 94-142 might just force this dream to become a reality.)

• All concerned groups must work together to lobby for "greatly increased levels of funding . . . from the U.S. Congress and from state legislatures." (There are some signs the Proposition 13 mentality is decreasing.)

• Consistent with the NEA's position in other regards, the Panel wants a Cabinet-level Department of Education. Its members argue that this is essential for the implementation of the mainstreaming ideal. (Mission accomplished!)

A Final Word

Will mainstreaming become a truly guiding concept? (This certainly appears to be the trend at this writing.) If so, how far will it go in shaping our educational practices and policies in the future? What will the schools and other educative settings and agencies look like in the year 2000? No doubt, your guess is as good as mine. I believe, however, that the above two professional practitioner groups, neither of which is known for its radical stands on educational innovation, have given us a flavor of the ferment that exists and of the changes that are needed.

In my view there is no guesswork that if P.L. 94-142 is even partially implemented on a large scale (full implementation is far from a foregone conclusion in my judgment), then classrooms and alternative approaches to learning will be very different than they are today. Not only exceptional children, but "unexceptional" ones as well, will receive a very special education.

My dream is that mainstreaming-normalization-deinstitutionalization of the handicapped will not only be a major step toward realizing the full potential of persons who are different in ways that have caused them to be the objects of prejudice and discrimination, but also that it will contribute to the personalization of schooling for all. A significant new impetus has been given to the continuing struggle for sound, equitable, and humane educational opportunities for all. I refuse to discredit the movement on the grounds that it is unrealistic and utopian. Indeed, I believe progress is already underway.

Since I am an academic in a research-oriented institution, it will come as no surprise that I want to close this glance at the future by suggesting that mainstreamiing ought to, and probably will, stimulate scholarly productivity and dissemination. Throughout this Bulletin enormously important issues have been identified—most of which have been with us for a long time—that demand further study: the nature of attitude change, the process of personalizing instruction, the nature of oppression of people who are different from ourselves, the role of conflict in decision making, and others.

In brief, I am greatly encouraged by this movement. I believe it is consistent with what many social studies educators have been promoting for years. I hope and trust that we rise to the challenge.

Footnotes

[1] Although it is generally supportive of P.L. 94-142, see *Education for All Handicapped Children: Consensus, Conflict and Challenge—A Study Report* of the National Education Association's Teacher Rights Division, 1978, for a variety of critical remarks by classroom teachers.

[2] McCoy Vernon, "The Road to Hell," *American Annals of the Deaf* (December, 1978): 913.

[3] See, for example, *Educating All the Handicapped—What the Laws Say and What Schools Are Doing*, National School Public Relations Association, 1977.

[4] For projections by members of advocacy groups working for handicapped pupils, see the doctoral dissertation by Janis Lynn Paushter, *A Study of Opinions on Predicted Future Events Affecting the Education of Handicapped Children, 1975-2000*, Columbia University-Teachers College, 1976.

For projections by a few leading scholars in the field of Special Education, see Maynard C. Reynolds, ed., *Future of Education for Exceptional Children: Emerging Structures*, University of Minnesota, National Support Systems Project, 1978. (Report of a conference on trends.)

[5] William V. Schipper and Leonard A. Kenowitz, *Special Education Futures: A Forecast of Events Affecting the Education of Exceptional Children*, National Association of State Directors of Special Education, 1975.

[6] *Education for All Handicapped Children* . . . *op. cit.*, pp 39-45.

". . . social studies professionals must modify, apply, adapt, or otherwise make their own bridges from theory to practice."

11.Representative Sources

To assist social studies teachers in mainstreaming, all the authors of this Bulletin submitted references—books, articles, and other sources— that they thought were of value to teachers. The editors processed and compiled these suggestions in order to provide a resource chapter to facilitate the preparation and/or implementation of mainstreaming. Where possible, annotations on the contents of the references are included. It is hoped that the collective experience and expertise of all the authors will provide direction and efficiency in exploring the path to the "least restrictive environment."

A review of the listings (and literature) reveals a paucity of materials that directly relate to social studies education. Therefore, social studies professionals must modify, apply, adapt, or otherwise make their own bridges from theory to practice. The literature and, it is hoped, this Bulletin provide generic information on systems, procedures, strategies, and materials that will support this process. Essentially, social studies teachers must develop their own applications for mainstreaming.

1. Print Materials

Adams, Anne H., Charles R. Coble, and Paul B. Hounshell. *Mainstreaming Language Arts and Social Studies.* Santa Monica, California: Goodyear Publishing Company, 1977.

Blackburn, J. E. and W. C. Powell. *One at a Time All at Once: The Creative Teacher's Guide to Individualized Instruction Without Anarchy.* Pacific Palisades, California: Goodyear, 1976.

Board of Cooperative Educational Services, Cayuga-Onondaga BOCES. *A Manual Outlining the Process Involved in the Development of the Individual Educational Plan as Prescribed in Federal and State Laws and Regulations.* Mark Costello, Director of Special Education. Auburn, New York: 1977. A mimeographed document.

Caplan, R. B. *Helping the Helpers to Help.* New York: The Seabury Press, 1972.

Center for Innovation in Teaching the Handicapped. *Bibliography of Mainstreaming Resource Materials.* Bloomington, Indiana: School of Education, Indiana University, 1978.

Center for Innovation in Teaching the Handicapped. *CITH Publications List.* Bloomington, Indiana: School of Education, Indiana University.

Center for Innovation in Teaching the Handicapped. *Directory of CITH Training Materials.* Bloomington Indiana: School of Education, Indiana University.

Christesen, Barbara. *Map Skills A, B, C, D.* New York: Scholastic Magazines, 1978.

    Task-analysed student materials focus on reading and interpreting map skills.

Council for Exceptional Children. *The Education for All Handicapped Act—P.L. 94-142.* Reston, Virginia: The Council for Exceptional Children, 1977.

Fenton, Edwin (ed.). *The Americans: A History of the United States.* New York: Holt, Rinehart and Winston, 1975.

    Developed at the Carnegie-Mellon University Social Studies Curriculum Development Center for slow learners in grades 7-8; text is accompanied by cassette phonotapes, 4 sets of 84 pictures, and test spirit masters.

Fenton, Edwin, ed. *Living in Urban America.* New York: Holt, Rinehart and Winston, 1974.

    Developed at the Carnegie-Mellon University Social Studies Curriculum Development Center for slow learners in grades 9-10.

Goldstein, Herbert. *Social Learning Curriculum, Primary Phases 1-10* and *Social Learning Curriculum, Intermediate Phases 11-16.* Columbus, Ohio: Charles E. Merrill Publishing Co., 1975.

Gregory, George. "Using the Newspaper in the Mainstreamed Classroom." *Social Education* 43 (February 1979): 140-43.

Hamill, D.D. "The Resource-Room Model in Special Education." *Journal of Special Education* 6 (4) (1972): 349-354.

Herlihy, John G. and Myra T. Herlihy, eds. "Mainstreaming: The Least Restrictive Environment." *Social Education* 43 (January 1979): 57-68.

    An entire elementary education section devoted to mainstreaming in elementary social studies. See also reference to Gregory article, *supra.*

Herman, W. L. "Reading and Other Language Arts in Social Studies Instruction: Persistent Problems." In R. C. Preston, ed. *A New Look at Reading in the Social Studies.* Newark, New Jersey: International Reading Association, 1969.

Hobbs, Nicholas, Nettie Bartel, Paul R. Dokecki, *et al. Exceptional Teaching for Exceptional Learning.* A Report to the Ford Foundation. New York: The Ford Foundation, 1979.

Johnson, R. and E. R. Vardian. "Reading, Readability, and the Social Studies." *The Reading Teacher* 26 (1973): 483-488.

Jordan, J. B., ed. *Teacher, Please Don't Close the Door—the Exceptional Child in the Mainstream.* Reston, Virginia: The Council for Exceptional Children, 1976.

Journal of Teacher Education XXIX, no. 6. (November-December 1978). Entire issue is devoted to various facets of mainstreaming.

Lowenbraun, Sheila and James Q. Affleck. *Teaching Mildly Handicapped Children in Regular Classes.* Columbus. Ohio: Charles E. Merrill, 1976.

Includes useful suggestions for mainstreaming in the classroom.

Mainstreaming: Origins and Implications. Minnesota Education. 2:2 (April 1976). University of Minnesota, College of Education.

Mainstreaming Training Systems, Materials and Resources: A Working List, (Part A), Mainstreaming: A Working Bibliography, (Part B). Minneapolis, Minnesota: National Support Systems Project, University of Minnesota, 1977.

A list of 900 published materials on mainstreaming (through October 1, 1977) was compiled. Components and purposes of each material or service are described and accompanied by names of publishers and addresses. (Free up to five copies; then $1.00 each).

Metsker, Carol assisted by Edith King. *Hints and Activities for Mainstreaming.* Dansville, New York: Instructor Publications, 1977.

Categorical approach stresses "how-to-do" classroom applications.

Meyen, Edward L., G. A. Vergason, and R. J. Whelan, eds. *Alternatives for Teaching Exceptional Children.* Denver: Love Publishing Company, 1975.

National Advisory Committee on the Handicapped. *The Individualized Education Program: Key to an Appropriate Education for the Handicapped Child, 1977 Annual Report.* Washington, D.C.: United States Government Printing Office, 1977.

National Education Association. *Education for All Handicapped Children: Consensus, Conflict and Challenge— A Study Report.* Washington, D.C.: National Education Association, 1978.

Though generally supportive, it contains critical remarks by teachers.

National Education Association. *Mainstreaming: What Teachers Say Series.* Washington, D.C.: National Education Association, 1977.

National Inservice Network. *Regular Education Inservice Projects: A Preliminary Description.* Bloomington, Indiana: School of Education, Indiana University, 1978.

O'Donnell, Patrick A. and Robert H. Bradfield, eds. *Mainstreaming: Controversy and Consensus.* San Rafael, California: Academic Therapy Publication, 1976.

Paushter, Janis Lynn. *A Study of Opinions on Predicted Future Events Affecting the Education of Handicapped Children, 1975-2000.* Doctoral dissertation. Teachers College, Columbia University, 1976.

Preparation of Regular Classroom Teachers for Work with Special Learning Problems: A Preservice Training Project. Greeley, Colorado: Special Education for Regular Teachers, School of Special Education and Rehabilitation, University of Northern Colorado.

Twenty-five separate units deal with topics appropriate for preparing regular classroom teachers to teach mainstreamed, mildly handicapped children. Unit 24—Social Studies for Children with Special Needs; Unit 25—Adapting Curricula for Handicapped Students at the Secondary Level. Contact: Dr. Clifford D. Baker at above address.

Project MAVIS (Materials Adaptations for Visually Impaired Students in the Social Studies). Boulder, Colorado: Social Science Education Consortium, Inc., 1979.

Titles are: *Resources for Teaching Social Studies in the Mainstreamed Classroom. Social Studies for the Visually Impaired Child. Important Concerns in the Education of Visually Impaired Children. Who Is the Visually Impaired child? Encouraging Successful Mainstreaming of the Visually Impaired Child. Teaching the Visually Impaired Child in the Regular Classroom.*

Readings in Mainstreaming, 78/79. Guilford, Connecticut: Special Learning Corporation, 1978.

Collection of periodical articles on many aspects of mainstreaming.

Reynolds, Maynard C., ed. *Future of Education for Exceptional Children: Emerging Structures.* University of Minnesota: National Support Systems Project, 1978.

Report of conference on trends in education for the handicapped.

Reynolds, Maynard C., ed. *Mainstreaming; Origins and Implications*. Reston, Virginia: The Council for Exceptional Children,1976.

Reynolds, Maynard C. and Jack W. Birch. *Teaching Exceptional Children in All America's Schools*. Reston, Virginia: The Council for Exceptional Children, 1977.

Comprehensive, up-to-date fundamental source by two key experts.

Sapon-Shevin, Mara. "Another Look at Mainstreaming: Exceptionality, Normality, and the Nature of Difference." *Phi Delta Kappan* 60:2 (October 1978): 119-21.

Strategies and Techniques for Mainstreaming—A Resource Room Handbook. Monroe, Michigan: Monroe County Intermediate School District.

Describes resource room models and includes "How-To"chapters.

Turnbull, Ann P. and Jane B. Schulz. *Mainstreaming Handicapped Students: A Guide for the Classroom Teacher*. Boston: Allyn and Bacon Inc., 1979.

Basic, concise source on all aspects of mainstreaming; first four chapters are an excellent introduction to mainstreaming.

Turner, T. N. "Making the Social Studies Textbook a More Effective Tool for Less Able Readers." *Social Education* 41 (January 1976): 38-41.

Watson, Marjorie. *Mainstreaming with Special Emphasis on the Educable Mentally Retarded*, revised edition. Washington, D.C.: National Education Association, 1977.

2. Audiovisual Materials

Approaches To Mainstreaming, Unit 1: Teaching the Special Child in the Regular Classroom.

This series of four sound filmstrips for inservice training provides information and practical suggestions to help regular classroom teachers meet the needs of special students in their classrooms. Teaching Resources Corporation, 100 Boylston Street, Boston, Massachusetts 68583. $69.00.

Approaches to Mainstreaming, Unit 2: Teaching the Special Child in the Classroom.

This series of four sound filmstrips for inservice training provides information and practical suggestions to help regular classroom teachers meet the needs of special students in their classrooms. Teaching Resources Corporation, 100 Boylston Street, Boston, Massachusetts 68583. $69.00.

Coming Back. . .Or Never Leaving: Instructional Programming for Handicapped Students in the Mainstream.

This package includes a text, trainer's guide, and series of five sound filmstrips that provide an introduction to the various aspects of mainstreaming and offer in-depth case studies. Charles E. Merrill Publishing Company, 1300 Alum Creek Drive, Columbus, Ohio 43216. $135.00—Media Package, $9.95— Text.

Controlling Classroom Misbehavior.

This filmstrip program suggests principles of behavior management and practical procedures that may be applied in the classroom. National Education Association Publications, Order Department, Academic Building, Saw Mill Road, West Haven, Connecticut 06516. $10.00

Council for Exceptional Children.

CEC has developed three multimedia packages to help educators and parents understand the many facets of P.L. 94-142. Included in the packages are three captioned filmstrips and three audio cassettes. 1. "Introducing P.L. 94-142," 2. "Complying with P.L. 94-142," 3. "P.L. 94-142 Works for Children." The Council for Exceptional Children, 1920 Association Dr., Reston, Virginia 22091.

The School Daze of the Learning Disability Child.

This filmstrip and cassette program enables the user to experience some of the difficulties school psychologists face in attempting to make a differential diagnosis for children with learning disabilities. It illustrates the difficult task the teacher has in overcoming the invisible barriers to learning. Alpern Communications,

220 Gulph Hills Road, Radnor, Pennsylvania 19087. $60.00

Scholastic Magazines, Inc. *Feeling Free Program*. New York: Scholastic Book Services, 1978.

A multimedia program including teacher guides, six student booklets, and films. This is a student instructional program.

"Coming Home"

"Graduation"

"Try Another Way"

For a description of these films and where they can be obtained, see Chapter 8.

3. Specialized Sources

"Talking books" and taped versions of social studies texts may be acquired from:

a. American Printing House for the Blind, 1839 Frankfurt Avenue, Louisville, Kentucky 40206.

b. Aids / Appliances Catalog, American Foundation for the Blind, 15 West 16 Street, New York, New York 10011.

c. State Libraries for the Blind

Captioned films and filmstrips for the deaf are available on a free loan basis from:

Captioned Films for the Deaf, Special Office for Materials Distribution, Indiana University Audio-Visual Center, Bloomington, Indiana 47401.

There are many community organizations (with national affiliations) that can aid the teacher to mainstream. They will vary with your geographic location, so no addresses are included. Check your telephone book. Some of these organizations are listed below:

American Foundation for the Blind

Association for Children with Learning Disabilities

Association for the Deaf

Association for Retarded Citizens

Council for Exceptional Children

Office of Vocational Rehabiltation

United Cerebral Palsy Association

Index

96

Index by Glenna Bergquist
Book design and production by Joseph Perez
Cover design by Bill Caldwell
Typography by Harwood Typographic Service
Printing by Edwards Brothers
Photos: pp. 2, 16, 42, 76 by Roger B. Smith,
    SUNY Geneseo; pp. 8, 22, 34, 52, 66, 82, 90
    by Joe Di Dio, National Education Association

OTHER NCSS PUBLICATIONS

HISTORY

TEACHING OF WORLD HISTORY
Gerald Leinwand
Focuses on ways to strengthen the World History course through curricular patterns, use of sources, and skills development.
90 pp. $5.50   1978

TEACHING AMERICAN HISTORY:
THE QUEST FOR RELEVANCY
Allan O. Kownslar, Editor
Specific, practical, and class-tested lessons designed to relate the American past to the needs of today's students.
237 pp. $6.95   1974

THE REINTERPRETATION OF
AMERICAN HISTORY AND CULTURE
William H. Cartwright and Richard L. Watson, Jr., Editors
Outstanding scholars discuss recent interpretations of American history from colonial times to the present.
554 pp. $8.50   1973

HISTORY PACKET—All materials in this group
$16.95

INTERNATIONAL

TEACHING SOCIAL STUDIES IN OTHER NATIONS
Howard D. Mehlinger and Jan L. Tucker, Editors
Up-to-date analysis of social studies education in England, the Federal Republic of Germany, Japan, Nigeria, and Thailand.
104 pp. $6.95   1979

INTERNATIONAL LEARNING AND INTERNATIONAL
EDUCATION IN A GLOBAL AGE
Richard C. Remy, James A. Nathan, James M. Becker, & Judith V. Torney
Examines ways to learn about the world, alternative views of the world, and designs for world studies programs. Bibliography and Guidelines.
104 pp. $5.50   1975

HOW-TO-DO-IT
Provides a practical and useful source of classroom methods and techniques for elementary and secondary teachers.

Series #1

HOW TO ASK QUESTIONS (#24)	$1.00
HOW TO USE SIMULATIONS (#25)	$1.00
HOW TO STUDY POLITICAL PARTICIPATION (#27)	$1.00
HOW TO TEACH ABOUT HUMAN BEINGS (#28)	$1.00
HOW-TO-DO-IT SERIES #1 Packet with Binder	$4.00

Series #2

IMPROVING READING SKILLS IN SOCIAL STUDIES (#1)	$1.00
EFFECTIVE USE OF FILMS IN SOCIAL STUDIES CLASSROOMS (#2)	$1.00
REACH FOR A PICTURE (#3)	$1.00
USING QUESTIONS IN SOCIAL STUDIES (#4)	$1.00
ARCHITECTURE AS A PRIMARY SOURCE FOR SOCIAL STUDIES (#5)	$1.00
PERSPECTIVES ON AGING (#6)	$1.00
CLASSROOM MANAGEMENT IN THE SOCIAL STUDIES (#7)	$1.00
ORAL HISTORY IN THE CLASSROOM (#8)	$1.00
USING POPULAR CULTURE IN THE SOCIAL STUDIES (#9)	$1.00
HOW-TO-DO-IT SERIES #2 Packet with binder	$9.00

CURRENT ISSUES
AND SPECIAL TOPICS

SCIENCE AND SOCIETY: KNOWING, TEACHING, LEARNING
Cheryl Charles & Bob Samples, Editors
Distinguished collection of essays by Fritjof Capra, Rollo May, Margaret Mead, Carl Rogers, Jonas Salk, and others.
88 pp. $4.95   1978

FUTURES UNLIMITED:
TEACHING ABOUT WORLDS TO COME
Robert M. Fitch & Cordell M. Svengalis
Provides a theoretical framework and practical suggestions for teachers planning to teach about the future.
88 pp. $6.95   1979

BUILDING RATIONALES FOR CITIZENSHIP EDUCATION
James P. Shaver, Editor
Perceptive examination of assumptions beneath decisions that affect citizenship education, and a search for a rationale.
118 pp. $4.95   1977

TEACHING ABOUT WOMEN IN THE SOCIAL STUDIES:
CONCEPTS, METHODS, AND MATERIALS
Jean Dresden Grambs, Editor
Valuable publication for teaching about women in U.S. History, World History, and other courses. Guidelines for selecting instructional materials.
119 pp. $5.95   1976

VALUES OF THE AMERICAN HERITAGE:
CHALLENGES, CASE STUDIES, AND TEACHING STRATEGIES
Carl Ubbelohde & Jack R. Fraenkel, Editors
Explores American values. Case studies of impressment of seamen, trial of Susan B. Anthony, Mormon experiences, and Standard Oil Company.
214 pp. $8.75   1976

CURRENT ISSUES—SPECIAL TOPICS PACKET—All materials in this group $30.00.

MULTIETHNIC

TEACHING ETHNIC STUDIES
James A. Banks, Editor
Outstanding yearbook with major sections on teaching about Asian Americans,
Blacks, Chicanos, Native Americans, and Puerto Ricans.
300 pp. $7.20   1973

CURRICULUM GUIDELINES FOR MULTIETHNIC EDUCATION
$2.50

MULTIETHNIC PACKET—All materials in this group
$9.00

ELEMENTARY

SOCIAL STUDIES IN EARLY CHILDHOOD:
AN INTERACTIONIST POINT OF VIEW
Alicia L. Pagano, Editor
Analyzes how young children develop through action, by solving problems, and
by contact with other children, parents, teachers, and the media.
96 pp. $4.95   1978

SOCIAL STUDIES AND THE ELEMENTARY TEACHER:
PROMISES AND PRACTICES
William W. Joyce and Frank L. Ryan, Editors
Anthology of stimulating articles on teaching methods, programs of study, and
instructional environments.
182 pp. $4.95   1977

Orders not on official P.O.'s must be prepaid. ALL ORDERS UNDER $10.00
MUST BE PREPAID. Make checks payable to:

NCSS
3615 Wisconsin Ave., N.W.
Washington, D.C. 20016